...nting Publications of Scholars Book Co.

ROBERT R. STERLING, EDITOR

...nder et al., *Five Monographs on Business Income*
...ray, *The Accounting Mission*
...ambers, *Accounting, Evaluation and Economic Behavior*
...Dickinson, *Accounting Practice and Procedure*
...eek, *Ancient Double-Entry Bookkeeping*
...atfield, *Accounting: Its Principles and Problems*
...on Hunt (Editor), *George Oliver May: Twenty-Five Years*
...nting Responsibility
...e *Foundations of Accounting Measurement*
...cNeal, *Truth in Accounting*
...essich, *Accounting and Analytical Methods*
...lay, *Financial Accounting*
...ntagna, *Certified Public Accounting: A Sociological View of*
...ssion in Change
...drew Paton, *Accounting Theory*
...Ripley, *Main Street and Wall Street*
...Schandl, *Theory of Auditing*
...*The Cultural Significance of Accounts*
... Simon et al., *Centralization vs. Decentralization in Organizing*
...ontroller's Department
...Sprague, *The Philosophy of Accounts*
...Staubus, *Making Accounting Decisions*
...Staubus, *A Theory of Accounting to Investors*
...R. Sterling (Editor), *Asset Valuation and Income Determination*
...R. Sterling (Editor), *Institutional Issues in Public Accounting*
...R. Sterling (Editor), *Research Methodology in Accounting*
...R. Sterling and William F. Bentz (Editors), *Accounting in Perspective*
...Storey, *The Search for Accounting Principles*
...Group on Business Income, *Changing Concepts of Business Income*

Accounting in Perspective

Contributions to Accounting Thought by Other Disciplines

Papers and Discussions from
Accounting Colloquium I
cosponsored by
The University of Kansas School of Business
and
The Arthur Young Foundation

Edited by

Robert R. Sterling
and
William F. Bentz

Scholars Book Co.
4431 Mt. Vernon
Houston, Texas 77006

Library of Congress Cataloging in Publication Data

Accounting Colloquium, 1st, University of Kansas, 1969.
   Accounting in perspective.

   Includes bibliographies.
   1. Accounting—Congresses. I. Sterling, Robert R.
II. Bentz, William F. III. Kansas. University.
School of Business. IV. Arthur Young Foundation.
V. Title.
[HF5603.A325   1969a]   657   78-26732
ISBN 0-914348-25-6

Printed in the United States of America

TABLE OF CONTENTS

PART I PHILOSOPHICAL AND METHODOLOGICAL ISSUES IN ACCOUNTING RESEARCH

v

PART II   EXPANDING PERSPECTIVES IN CONTEMPORARY ACCOUNTING RESEARCH

PART III   PROBLEMS IN THE IMPLEMENTATION OF ACCOUNTING RESEARCH

FOREWORD

The word "accounting" is used to describe an extremely complex function. Supporting the accounting function, and to a large extent comprising it, are elements which are shared by other disciplines. Among these elements are the theories of mathematics and measurement, information and communication, economics and sociology, and human behavior.

To get a man to the moon took the coordinated application of mathematics, astronomy, medicine, physics, engineering, chemistry, nutrition, and aerodynamics. Knowledge expands, and its conventional categories become inadequate. Thought takes new directions. There are new ways of looking at old subjects. There are new arrangements of information, and changes in perspective and focus. Specialists cross each other's paths. The network of knowledge becomes ever more complex.

Anticipating the interdisciplinary atmosphere which we can expect to see increasingly in the 1970s, the University of Kansas School of Business and the Arthur Young Foundation cosponsored Accounting Colloquium I, "Accounting in Perspective." Held at the University of Kansas in April 1969, Colloquium I brought together some seventy invited participants who represented the universities, regulatory agencies, corporate business, and public accounting. The spirit of this Colloquium was inquiry. Participants were encouraged to inquire into one another's disciplines—to question, explore and understand the phenomena, the premises, the theories, and the methodologies. Particularly sought after was an understanding of the contributions that were being made to accounting thought by other disciplines. Invited to address these seventy representative accountants were some of America's outstanding thinkers. Each brought to the Colloquium the special insights of his own discipline, but applied the insights to the varied concerns of accounting. Selected addresses are now made available for the reader so that he too may share in these interdisciplinary aspects of accounting.

STANLEY P. PORTER
Arthur Young & Company

Dallas, Texas

INTRODUCTION

The conference subtitle, "Contributions to Accounting Thought by Other Disciplines," provides some insight into the planned thrust of the program. Although some of the links between accounting and other disciplines are seemingly apparent, many links may not be so obvious. For example, the relevance of economic theory has long been recognized in accounting research and curricula. However, the study of measurement theory has not been widespread in accounting even though accountants purport to measure things. Further, it has been said that accountants practice a utilitarian art which includes the communication of information about economic events. If so, then information theory and the behavioral aspects of communication are linked to accounting thought. This conference was organized so that scholars from various disciplines could congregate in order to explore the links between accounting and the other disciplines represented.

The authors responded to the conference theme in various ways. Professors Yuji Ijiri and C. West Churchman concern themselves with the role of accounting in society and in the firm, as well as with fundamental issues of research methodology.

Professors Selwyn Becker, Paul F. Lazarsfeld and Baruch Lev are concerned with the expansion of accounting into other disciplines. Included in their papers are some suggestions as to new directions in research, as well as some criticisms of past efforts.

Professors Solomon Fabricant and Ezra Solomon are concerned with the specific research topics of price-level changes and the measurement of rate of return, respectively.

Professor Ijiri provides some very useful insights into the role of accounting theory development as it relates to accounting practice and to accounting policy, as set forth by a group such as the Accounting Principles Board. In addition, Ijiri reviews the two approaches to language: logical empiricism and ordinary language philosophy. Once the distinction has been made between the deductive approach to theory construction and the inductive approach, Ijiri discusses logical analysis as a method for constructing theory in accounting. Ijiri's paper, with comments by Professors Robert E. Jensen and Claude S. Colantoni, provides a much-needed perspective of accounting research, as well as providing an extensive explanation of the deductive, or axiomatic approach to theory construction.

Professor Churchman raises "the question of whether it is possible to convert some sections of accounting practice into something that begins to approximate a measurement system." To illustrate the measurement issue, Churchman contrasts the measurement processes used in the physical sciences with the data gathering processes used in the social sciences. He concludes that accountants do not measure because measurement "is the very refined relationship between theory and observation," and accounting data is collected without recognizing that relationship.

Churchman's remarks are intended to provoke some thought and study of the measurement process by accounting researchers. In raising the measurement issue, Churchman reveals his view of the role of accounting in the business firm. This view of accounting clearly has significant implications with respect to the direction of future accounting research. Some of these implications are discussed by Professors William W. Cooper and Kermit D. Larson.

Professor Becker's paper, when combined with the commentaries of Professors Andrew C. Stedry and William J. Bruns, Jr., provides the outline of a behavioral problem in accounting research. Becker evaluates "behavioral" research in accounting and finds many limitations and faults in the work of many accounting researchers. His criticisms are useful in the process of interpreting the significance of past research in the behavioral aspects of accounting, as well as the reliability of the conclusions drawn in those studies.

In a more positive vein, Becker, a psychologist, suggests that accountants become concerned with the development of "middle range theory," which he outlines in sufficient detail to be of some general guidance in future research.

Professors Bruns and Stedry raise an important behavioral issue in the process of commenting on Becker's paper. Given the training of many scholars in accounting, the use of the knowledge and methodologies from other disciplines involves some risk, and will continue to be risky until accounting researchers become better trained in basic research. An explicit understanding of the benefits and penalties of interdisciplinary research is important if one is attempting to influence the direction of research in accounting. Topics once considered to be outside the purview of accounting are now being accepted as scholarly research in accounting, but only after some struggle.

Professor Lazarsfeld explores some areas into which the accounting profession may want to expand. The implications for accounting research are clear, because extensive research and the development of teaching material will have to precede accounting practice in the suggested areas of expansion.

In contrast to the general suggestions of Lazarsfeld, Professor Lev applies information theory concepts to a specific accounting problem, the analysis of financial statements. It serves as a specific application, in accounting, of theory developed in another discipline.

Professor Fabricant provides some arguments and persuasive evidence in support of his contention that financial statements should be adjusted for price-level changes. His paper includes an extensive discussion of the price-level issue as well as a discussion of price index construction. Professors Maurice Moonitz and Paul Rosenfield provide some interesting comments and insights as to why accounting practice may be lagging in the price-level problem.

The problem of measuring rate of return on investment is reviewed by Ezra Solomon. This problem has received continued attention in the literature of accounting and finance for many years. Solomon's paper, plus the commentaries of Professors George J. Staubus and Myron J. Gordon, provide useful information and suggestions for those researchers currently interested in measures of the rate of return.

It is a pleasure to acknowledge our debt to our many friends and alumni in Arthur Young & Company. In addition to financial support — the Colloquium was made possible by a grant from the Arthur Young Foundation — they were most generous with their time and talent. Special thanks are due to Stanley P. Porter for his long-standing support of and interest in the University as well as his invaluable assistance with the Colloquium; to John J. Schornack for assistance in planning and organizing the Colloquium; and to Albert Newgarden for editorial advice and assistance.

Finally, our thanks to our former colleague, George Sorter, who served as co-chairman of the Colloquium.

R.R.S.
W.F.B.

Lawrence, Kansas

PART 1
Philosophical and Methodological Issues
in Accounting Research

LOGIC AND SANCTIONS
IN ACCOUNTING

Yuji Ijiri

'I don't know what you mean by "glory,"' Alice said. Humpty
Dumpty smiled contemptuously. 'Of course, you don't — till I
tell you. I meant "there's a nice knock-down argument for you!"'
'But "glory" doesn't mean "a nice knock-down argument,"'
Alice objected.
'When *I* use a word,' Humpty Dumpty said in rather a scornful
tone, 'it means just what I choose it to mean — neither more nor
less.'
'The question is,' said Alice, 'whether you *can* make words
mean so many different things.'
'The question is,' said Humpty Dumpty, 'which is to be master
— that's all.'

L. Carroll, *Through the Looking Glass*

INTRODUCTION

"Which is to be master?" It seems that in this question lies a
key to understanding the nature of accounting, a system for communicating economic events of an entity.

Like any other language, accounting has a complicated set of
rules on how one may express economic events of an entity. These
rules are aimed at serving people; but, on the other hand, people are
constrained by them. Unless people sacrifice their freedom and observe
the rules, accounting cannot serve them. Thus, people play a dual
role in accounting; they are the master and at the same time the servants
of accounting. Although this dual role of people is observable in
many social systems, it is particularly important in understanding
accounting in its social context, in establishing policies on how accounting should be changed, and in implementing the policies by
changing accounting practices. For this reason, we would like to
explore the interaction of people and accounting in this paper. In
doing so, we would like to keep two factors in mind — that is, logic
and sanctions of accounting.

In section two the triad of accounting theories, policies, and practices will be analyzed. It is particularly crucial for us to understand the relationships among these three factors in the field of accounting, since accounting theories are likely to be mixed up with accounting policies, accounting policies are likely to be mixed up with accounting practices, and vice versa. Section three is devoted to the logical analyses in linguistics. Accounting and linguistics have a great many similarities. The issues on the logical approaches in linguistics, especially logical empiricism versus ordinary language philosophy, are quite relevant to our problems in accounting.

In section four we discuss logical analyses in accounting by means of a formal axiomatic system in mathematical logic. Logical deduction from such an axiomatic accounting system can suggest interchanges of ideas developed over different types of assets. As an example, "FIFO or LIFO depreciation methods" as well as "declining-balance inventory valuation methods" are discussed in section five together with their potential uses and problems in implementation.

Section six reviews the sanctions in accounting which make the field of accounting quite different from the field of linguistics where such sanctions are not granted. It analyzes the logic in legal reasoning which has a significant impact on accounting practices by providing rules of interpreting accounting policies set up by the policy makers.

The last section, section seven, closes the paper with an emphasis on two entirely different roles played by accounting theorists and accounting policy makers which are likely to be mixed together in the accounting issues.

THE TRIAD OF ACCOUNTING THEORIES, POLICIES, AND PRACTICES

The field of accounting is a mixture of many elements from what accountants actually do to what they say they ought to do, from current topics to historical investigations, and from day-to-day practices to metaphysical observations of theories. In understanding the field of accounting, however, it appears to be useful to consider the relationships of three of its main elements: accounting theories, policies, and practices.

It is clear that accounting practices are the basic objects of studies for formulating accounting theories and policies. They are like our daily conversations in linguistics, actual weather in meteorology, or chemical reactions in chemistry. Contrary to the concept of accounting practices, the concepts of accounting theories and policies are rather ambiguous, requiring a clarification before we proceed.

When we say theories in linguistics, meteorology, or chemistry, we feel that all of these fields have something in common. That is, they are all derived from empirical observations by means of the process of abstraction. In the process of abstraction, the scientists do not make a value judgment as to what the empirical phenomena ought to be. Their objective in building theories is to explain a huge volume of observations by an organized set of concepts. Whether or not these phenomena are desirable for the welfare of human beings is irrelevant in the theory-building process.

The corresponding theory-building process in accounting will then be seen as a process of abstracting from a mass of observations of accounting practices without arguing whether or not they ought to be different from what they are. We accept them as they are and try to develop theories which will describe a maximum volume of observations by the simplest set of concepts, just like the attempt by linguists to develop grammar.

However, the field of accounting contains another important element, accounting policies. Contrary to the fields of linguistics, meteorology, or chemistry, accountants can change their practices relatively easily. As we shall be seeing later, the Accounting Principles Board is given an authority to maintain or change the current accounting practices. Therefore, it becomes an essential problem for accountants to know how accounting practices should be developed in the future. This is the area of accounting policies. Accounting policy-makers utilize the results of the work by accounting theorists and make decisions on how accounting practices ought to be changed based on their value judgment, upon which the decisions are implemented in practice.

These three areas of accounting — theories, policies, and practices — form a triad which may be represented by a diagram as follows:

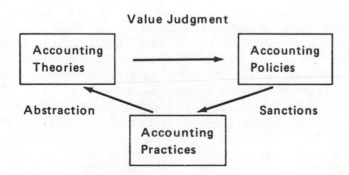

Figure 1. An Accounting Triad

The sanctions by which accounting policies become implemented are quite essential in understanding the field of accounting, since it is possible to change practices to fit theories! This is unthinkable for scientists in other fields for whom the empirical phenomena are almighty: no matter how beautiful and elegant the theory may be, if it does not fit the empirical phenomena, it is replaced by one which fits better.

Because of these close relationships among theories, policies, and practices, it is natural that in many cases one accountant plays a role of a theorist, a role of a policy-maker, and a role of a practitioner, simultaneously or in sequence. As a result, the distinction between theories and policies often becomes unclear. As we shall discuss in the concluding section of this paper, the distinction between the two is important because of the different degrees of objectivity required in theories and policies. We shall repeat that what we mean by accounting theories are statements abstracted from accounting practices. Of course, accounting theories may be aimed at disclosing what current practices do not do, or they may take the form of "if such and such hold (are desirable, necessary) then such and such need to be done (should not be done) in current accounting practices."[1] However, we shall exclude any expressions on "what ought to be" from our consideration of accounting theories.

Having separated accounting theories from accounting policies, we are ready to examine the role of logical analyses in the process of constructing theories from practices. However, it may be worthwhile to review the role of logical analyses in linguistics because of the similarity between the field of accounting and the field of linguistics.

LOGICAL ANALYSES IN LINGUISTICS

Accounting is a language in business. Various business phenomena are expressed in accounting records and reports and are communicated to others, as our daily phenomena are recorded, reported, and communicated to others by an ordinary language such as English. Accounting has its own rules of coding the phenomena, as does an ordinary language. Deviations from the accepted rules are punished implicitly or explicitly both in accounting and in an ordinary language. On the other hand, these rules are flexible enough to accommodate changing environment in business or in culture. Because of these

---

[1]It is, of course, possible to consider the process of value judgment by accounting policy-makers as objects of a study and develop theories about them. However, they will not be discussed in this paper due to their different characteristics from the standpoint of logical analyses. For example, see the work by Churchman [7].

similarities in the objects of the study, it is interesting to see how logical analyses have been made in linguistics.[2]

Katz discusses the two dominant movements in twentieth-century philosophy of language, namely *logical empiricism* and *ordinary language philosophy*.[3] The approach and the objective of the logical empiricists can perhaps be best explained by the following statements by Carnap, a leading spokesman for logical empiricism.

> The fact that natural languages [such as English or accounting — Y. I.] allow the formation of meaningless sequences of words [such as 'Profit is a moon,' or 'Dr. Capital stock $15: Cr. Head Office $15' — Y. I.] without violating the rules of grammar, indicates that grammatical syntax is, from the logical point of view, inadequate. If grammatical syntax corresponds exactly to logical syntax, pseudo-statements (statements having an apparently acceptable grammatical form but conveying no cognitive meaning) could not arise. . . .It follows that if our thesis that the statements of metaphysics are pseudo-statements is justifiable, then metaphysics could not even be expressed in a logically constructed language. This is the great philosophical importance of the task, which at present occupies the logicians, of building a logical syntax.[4]

With this objective, the logical empiricists constructed what they considered to be an ideal artificial language based on formal logic. Katz's [19, p. 95] criticism of this approach goes as follows:

> . . . the logical empiricists were content to assume that they pretty much knew everything there is to know about language on the basis of traditional, schoolbook grammar. Beyond this, it was just a matter of inventing conventions or carrying out operationalistic investigations of speech behavior . . . and, although logical empiricism constructed general theories, it confined its efforts to highly arbitrary and conceptually impoverished theories about a class of artificial languages whose structure bears little similarity to the structure of natural languages.

Contrary to the "top-down" approach based upon a well-structured logical language, *ordinary language philosophers* took the "grass-root" approach starting with natural languages, however unstructured and unsystematic they may be. Again according to Katz [19, p. 69]:

---

[2]Compared with the several decades of development in the philosophy of language by a considerable number of people, the development of the philosophy of accounting does not appear to have attracted much attention except by a relatively small number of people. For example, see Bedford and Dopuch [3], Deinzer [8, pp. 42-54], Devine [9, pp. 104-28], Dopuch [10], and Hendriksen [14, pp. 6-7].

[3]J. J. Katz [19].

[4]R. Carnap [5, p. 68, and 4].

What ordinary language philosophy urged instead was that natural languages are perfectly all right as they stand so long as they are used properly, i.e., in the ordinary way. Conceptual confusions are consequences of aberrations in usage. . . .Thus, it is unnecessary to try to state linguistic conventions with full formal precision in an artificial language to correct aberrations in usage. Such corrections should be accomplished by a form of philosophical therapy and analysis which differs from that practiced by logical empiricists by concentrating on the descriptions of linguistic facts.

In this way, "The logical empiricist's approach regards a natural language as an imperfect approximation to some ideal language, which it is the logician's job to construct," [19, p. 75] while ordinary language philosophers argue, as Wittgenstein states:

> But here the word 'ideal' is liable to mislead, for it sounds as if these languages were better, more perfect, than our everyday language . . . as if it took the logician to show people at last what a correct sentence looked like.[5]

Katz's criticism of the approach by the ordinary language philosophers goes as follows:

> Ordinary language philosophers assumed they did not know anything systematic about the nature of language. But without such a theory they had no notion of the sort of system within which to represent linguistic facts and no motivated way of philosophizing from such facts. Their presentations of facts about English were thus informal and unorganized, so that the body of facts which they brought to light consisted of an unmanageably large assortment of heterogeneous data of undetermined philosophical relevance. . . .The comparison with Babylonian astronomy or Greek geometry before Euclid comes most readily to mind.[6]

Although our objectives of logical analyses of accounting language are different from those of linguists mentioned above, these two entirely different approaches are quite suggestive to accounting theorists. Should we be concerned with the details in the current accounting practices at the risk of ending up with Babylonian-astronomy type accounting theories? Or should we start with a highly logical accounting structure at the risk of being called unrealistic or impractical? These are the questions we must seriously consider in making logical analyses in accounting. Certainly, the experiences that linguists have acquired over a considerable period of time are worth looking into for accounting theorists before investing a large amount of valuable time

---

[5]L. Wittgenstein [31, p. 38e].
[6][19, pp. 94-5, 88].

resources. Controversies like those between logical empiricists and ordinary language philosophers will perhaps arise in accounting and will have to be resolved in regard to the issues of separating (more) objective expressions from (more) subjective expressions in accounting, or similarly in regard to the issues of relevancy.[7]

After criticizing the logical empiricism and the ordinary language philosophy, Katz proposes an approach which lies between the two. He recognizes that regularities observed in natural languages have varying degrees of generality; some can be considered as universal rules, while some hold only locally. While the logical empiricists tried to regard all rules as being universal and the ordinary language philosophers tried to regard all rules as being local, Katz regards the hierarchy of the degrees of generality as being an important characteristic of the regularities.

> A rough, but only a rough, analogy is this: Just as in some poker games we lay a card face up on the table and have it serve as a wild card in every player's hand, so that each hand actually consists of the cards dealt plus this wild card, we consider the theory of language to be part of every linguistic description, so that each such description consists of an account of the idiosyncratic facts about language. . . .In this way, linguistics achieves a high order of theoretical economy by avoiding the redundancy that would ensue if each truth about all languages were stated independently for each language . . . The more facts about particular languages that are found to be instances of general truths about language and are formulated as such, the tighter are the constraints imposed on systems that qualify as linguistic descriptions. The farther we thus empirically limit the logically possible diversity in natural languages, the richer the theory of universal structure given in the theory of language.[8]

This approach appears to be most useful for accounting theorists who analyze accounting practices. The practices in accounting are not always logically set up. Those dealing with inventories do not necessarily have the same principle as those dealing with fixed assets. Exceptional rules are often made and applied. The practices in different companies can differ and those in the same company can also differ over a period of time. Faced with such a diverse collection of practices, accounting theorists who attempt to describe them by a set of localized rules (some for receivables, some for inventories, and some for fixed assets) without exploring the uniform rules applicable to all of them,

---

[7]See [18] for the discussion on the degree of objectivity and subjectivity in accounting statements.
[8][19, pp. 109-10].

may be compared with the ordinary language philosophers. Those who attempt to describe them by a set of uniform rules, claiming their system as being superior to the existing one and hence often making a policy statement that accounting ought to be such and such, may be compared with the logical empiricists.

What we need is a hierarchical organization of rules, differentiating uniform rules from local ones. In this sense, logical analyses of accounting practices must be done with a greater care. The central question is no longer whether a rule is applicable or not, but to what extent it is applicable. Furthermore, before we decide on the range of applicability, we should try to exhaust all similarities and differences among the rules by asking why they are applicable as they are, in order to develop more general rules from them.

But what is the significance of making rules or theories more general? What advantages are there? These questions are related with the concept of the "simplicity" of a theory, since if we do not require some degree of "simplicity" in the theory, it is always possible to derive a general theory by simply adjoining local theories.

In introducing an inductive card game called "Eleusis," Martin Gardner states:

> It is an important insight into scientific method to realize that many hypotheses can be formulated to explain a given set of facts, and that any hypothesis can always be patched up, so to speak, to fit new facts that contradict it . . . Many a scientific hypothesis (e.g., the Ptolemaic model of the universe) has been elaborated to a fantastic degree in efforts to accommodate embarrassing new facts before it finally gave way to a simpler explanation. All of which raises two profound questions in the philosophy of science: why is the simplest hypothesis the best choice? How is 'simplicity' defined?[9]

An answer to the first question seems to lie not only in the economy or parsimony of concepts, or in the aesthetic value, but in providing a larger base for prediction, following our fundamental belief that theories observed more often in the past will be subject to less changes. If a theory A is applicable only in area G, and a theory B is applicable in another area H, which covers not only G, but goes beyond that, we consider B to be more stable than A and we rely more upon the prediction based on the theory B than one based on the theory A because B has a broader empirical base than does A. In accounting practices also, local theories are likely to be changed as easily as local conditions are changed, but uniform theories are unlikely to be changed because their changes require a complete remodeling of

---

9M. Gardner [12, p. 173].

the entire accounting system. For this reason, it is essential to have a hierarchical organization of accounting theories.

LOGICAL ANALYSES IN ACCOUNTING

One way to achieve such a hierarchical organization of accounting theories is to start with the existing accounting practices and go through the process of abstraction, eliminating locality at each step as it becomes necessary. Another approach is to start with the most uniform factor and then add localities as we approach the empirical phenomena. The former is similar to the approach by the ordinary language philosophers and the latter by the logical empiricists. However, the approaches presented here differ from the ordinary language philosophers and the logical empiricists in the sense that we are interested in developing a hierarchical organization of theories as described in the previous section.

There have been a large number of studies by accounting theorists who have contributed to the development of the theory of accounting.[10] However, an approach to the development of the accounting theory by means of an axiomatic system in mathematical logic has a different dimension of contribution. Below we shall elaborate.

> An axiomatic system is given by the specification of four things: A *vocabulary* that lists the symbols to be employed in the system, a set of *formation rules* that determine which strings of symbols in the vocabulary are syntactically acceptable as formulas of the system, i.e., as well-formed formulas, a set of *axioms* that comprise the unproven, true, well-formed formulas of the system, and a set of *inference rules* that determine the set of theorems with respect to the set of axioms.[11]

The vocabulary of accounting practices is a subset of the vocabulary of our ordinary language such as English. However, if we consider only journal entries and their subsequent recording in ledgers in the traditional manner, the vocabulary is limited to "Dr.", "Cr.", dates, account names, amounts, and a few other symbols such as ",", ".", ":", "$", although in actual entries there may be some descriptions of the transactions in the ordinary language. Then, so far as journal entries are concerned, the formation rule is:

---

[10]Notable contributions include American Accounting Association, *A Statement of Basic Accounting Theory* [1], N. M. Bedford [2], R. J. Chambers [6], C. T. Devine [9], E. O. Edwards and P. W. Bell [11], P. Grady [13], A. C. Littleton [23], R. Mattessich [25], M. Moonitz [26], W. A. Paton and A. C. Littleton [28], R. T. Sprouse and M. Moonitz [29], W. J. Vatter [30], and others.

[11]Katz [19, pp. 24-25]. Also, see Kleene [21].

"Dr." followed by a finite sequence of sets of an account name and an amount, then followed by "Cr." followed by another finite sequence of sets of an account name and an amount, providing the sums of all amounts in both sequences should be equal.

Thus "Dr. Cash $1,000 Cr. Accounts Payable $1,000" is a well-formed formula in the axiomatic system and so is "Dr. Land $5,000 Building $4,000 Cr. Cash $9,000." Such a formation rule plays an important role in computerizing the accounting processes.

Note that the formation rule tells us simply whether or not a formula is grammatically correct and does not tell us whether such a formula is true (or synonymously, valid). For example, in the propositional calculus if A and B are well-formed formulas then "A or B" (denoted by A∪B), "A and B" (denoted by A∩B), "A implies B" (denoted by A⊃B), "A is equivalent to B" (denoted by A~B), "not A" (denoted by ¬A), are all well-formed formulas according to the formation rule.[12] However, the formation rule does not tell us anything about the validity of these formulas. Similarly, in accounting journal entries, "Dr. Capital Stock $15 Cr. Head Office $15" is a well-formed formula, but the formation rule does not tell us whether such a transaction has actually occurred or even whether it is possible for such a transaction to occur.

The validity of formulas is determined by the axioms and the inference rules. A formula is considered to be valid if, and only if, it is either an axiom or is derived from the axioms and/or other valid formulas by applying the inference rules.

In the propositional calculus, some examples of axioms are A ⊃ (B⊃A), A⊃ (A∪B), and ¬¬ A⊃A.[13] Also the inference rule is the so-called *modus ponens* which says that B is provable from A and A⊃B, hence B is valid if A and A⊃B are both valid.[14]

Corresponding axioms and inference rules have been developed in accounting by Ijiri for the conventional accounting valuation based on historical cost.[15] The three axioms which are reproduced below from [16] are, more precisely, axiom schemata, since they specify judgment rules such that journal entries obtained by following these rules are considered to be valid. The valuation rules described in [16, Chapter 4] are reproduced below and correspond to the inference rules in the axiomatic system discussed above. They specify how

[12]See R. Carnap [5, p. 5].
[13]More precisely these are axiom schemata which become axioms when A and B are substituted by some definite propositions.
[14]Katz [19, pp. 33-34]. The validity and provability are equivalent in the propositional calculus. See Kleene [21, p. 43].
[15]They were originally reported in [15] and then revised in [16, Chapters 3 and 4].

valid journal entries may be prepared from the axioms and other valid journal entries.

AXIOMS

Axiom of Control: There exists a method by which resources under the control (present or future, positive or negative) of a given entity at any time t are uniquely determined at that time or later.

Axiom of Quantities: There exists a method by which all resources are uniquely partitioned into a collection of classes so that for each class a non-negative and additive quantity measure is defined and so that we are indifferent to any two sets of resources in the same class if and only if their quantities are the same.

Axiom of Exchanges: There exists a method by which all changes in the resources controlled by a given entity up to any time t are identified at that time later and are partitioned uniquely into an ordered set of pairs of an increment and a decrement, where the increment belongs to one and only one class.

VALUATION RULES

Basic Valuation Rule 1:   The value of any set of (present and future) resources in the basic class is defined to be equal to its quantity as determined by the quantity measure for the class.

Basic Valuation Rule 2:   The value of an empty set is defined to be equal to zero.

Value Allocation Rule: Allocate the value of all resources in each class before the exchange to outgoing resources in the class, and remaining resources in the class in proportion to their quantities.   The sum of values allocated to outgoing resources in each class is the value of the decrement.   Decrease the value of resources in each class by the value allocated to outgoing resources in the class.

Value Imputation Rule: If the resources in the increment belong to a nonbasic class, set the value of the increment equal to the value of the decrement.   Increase the value of resources of the class by the value of the increment.

Value Comparison Rule: If the resources in the increment belong to the basic class, calculate a value gain or loss by subtracting the value of the decrement from the value of the increment.

How were these axioms and valuation rules derived? They were derived by observing a large volume of journal entries and by trying to reduce them into a small set of categories. In this process, the set theory was very helpful, since it forces one to start from scratch. The set theory is in a sense mathematics for reconstruction, since it destroys all existing empirical relationship, retaining only the identifiability of basic elements and then reconstructs relationships among elements as we need them.   This is contrary to other branches of mathematics where variables are often assumed to have certain characteristics.

It is certainly possible to adopt the approach taken by the ordinary language philosophers. Namely, we start with collecting numerous accounting practices concerning asset valuation, and then simplify the data by classifying them according to the types of assets, such as cash, receivables, inventories, prepayments, and fixed assets.   For each class of assets, we can then develop a system of asset valuation, such as FIFO and LIFO for inventory valuation, and depreciation methods for fixed assets. Although we can step further in our process of logical induction, we are likely to stop here under this approach since the valuation methods for inventories and fixed assets seem to be based on entirely different principles. Actually, they appear to have been developed in practice without considering the mutual relationship at all.   However, the fact that they have been developed differently does not necessarily mean that we must consider them differently in developing accounting theories. Nevertheless, we must admit that it is rather difficult to imagine that both inventory valuation methods and depreciation methods can be explained by a simple unifying theory.

Here, the set theory can be very helpful in breaking away our conceptual boundaries.   Instead of considering each type of asset separately, we try to represent all assets by a set of points (or by a set of sets if necessary). In associating assets with points on a sheet of paper, we often find that our concept of assets is ambiguous. Precisely what is associated with a given point in our thinking is often vague, especially in the case of intangible assets. In any case, after some struggling, suppose we have represented each of the assets of a firm by a unique point on a sheet of paper. In doing so, we have eliminated all physical and economic characteristics of the assets, leaving only their identity and the fact that they all belong to the firm with which we are concerned.

This latter point gives rise to a significant operation we have just performed. That is, we have in effect separated the assets of the firm from the assets of all other entities. We have just defined a subset of the set of all economic resources.

What makes it possible for accountants to recognize certain resources as belonging to the firm and others not? What are the criteria for the selection? These questions are naturally highlighted once we attempt to carry out our analysis by the set theory. This is because all other factors are eliminated as being secondary.

At this stage we must go back to the pile of practices to see what actually makes accountants decide on this issue. We will then realize that there are two types of assets, those which the firm legally owns and those which represent only the rights by which the firm can enforce deliveries of resources. On the latter type of assets, we soon realize that only monetary rights are recorded and reported, while rights to receive goods or services are not. Thus, we notice that the criteria that accountants use in determining which assets the firm owns consist of two groups, one on the criteria dealing with assets that actually belong to the firm (called the control criteria) and the other on the criteria dealing with the conditions under which the assets the firm expects to receive in the future may be recognized as the assets of the firm at present (called the recognition criteria). Since the obligations to deliver goods and services are recorded and reported as liabilities, it becomes of interest to us to see whether the same criteria are applied for both receivables and payables of assets. The answer is "yes" as elaborated in [16]. This is a sequence of questions that arises when we analyze our problem by the set theory. From answers to these questions the Axiom of Control finally was established.

What else do accountants have to know (other than which assets belong to the firm) in order to value assets as they do in their practices? In practice, accountants do not deal with assets in the aggregate but rather, they classify assets based on their physical characteristics. Which physical characteristics? Again by observing the practices carefully, we soon recognize that they are based on the notion of indifference. If accountants think that generally people are indifferent between A and B, then they are put into the same class.

This creates a new problem — that is, indifference presupposes quantities. We must somehow snatch the concept of quantities from somewhere. Where does it come from? Does it exist independently from the valuation problem with which we are concerned, or is it dependent upon valuation? How do men learn the idea of quantities? What are their mathematical properties? How do accountants actually use these quantities in physical units in developing monetary valuation methods?

The attempt to understand the fundamental operations of accountants' minds in carrying out the classification and the measurement generated a host of these questions to be answered. Again, we must go back to the practices to see how accountants actually operate. The answers are summarized in the Axiom of Quantities.

These two axioms summarize the fundamental operations that enable accountants to define the assets of a firm, classify them, and represent them by a set of physical quantities. However, accountants need something else in order to develop monetary values of assets. How can they do it? A careful study of the practices indicates that the process is based on the concept of cost based on the operations called exchanges. When the firm obtains an asset A in exchange for an asset B, the monetary value of A is set equal to the monetary value of B which is derived internally from the accounting system at the time of the exchange. This requires the ability by the accountants to recognize which increase in the assets of the firm is causally related with which decrease in the assets. This is a far more advanced ability than those set forth in the previous two axioms. Therefore, a third axiom, Axiom of Exchanges, was established for this purpose.

In carrying through the valuation based on cost, we see that the problem of joint cost allocation occurs in many areas of accounting practice. For example, if two different types of assets, C and D, are obtained in exchange for asset E whose monetary value is $1,000, how should we allocate the $1,000 cost to C and D? In going through various practices, we see that there are no methods that are consistently applied through all occasions. Nevertheless, they are solved by some local rules. Thus, the Axiom of Exchanges requires that accountants be able to partition any exchange into a set of exchanges, each having only one type of asset as the asset increased by the exchange.

What else do we need? A further study of the practices showed that these three axioms more or less summarized the basic judgment accountants make, and the rest of what they do is quite routine and can be computerized if necessary. These three axioms are not an exhaustive list of all types of accountants' judgments. Here, the approach differs from that of logical empiricists. We admit that the list is incomplete, missing such types of judgment as one on reverse exchanges or cost-or-market-whichever-is-lower methods. However, we are hoping that these three axioms are necessary and sufficient to describe a majority of accounting practices on journal entries and asset valuation.[16]

The last step is to summarize the valuation rules observed in accounting practices, the routine part of journalizing after judgments by accountants have been made. Needless to say, these valuation rules are the core of the procedures for the historical cost accounting.

An axiomatic system in accounting has been constructed roughly in the way described above. Thus, the most fundamental rules of accounting practices have been systematized. Such an axiomatic

---

[16]See the discussions on this point in [16, Chapter 4].

system has not only a pedagogical value in teaching accounting practices in the simplest way but also, as emphasized before, a predictive value in deciding what kinds of practices are likely to remain over a longer period of time. Since these axioms summarize the essential factors in current practices, any changes in the axioms are likely to bring a fundamental change in current practices, unlike ad hoc modifications of practices which we often observe. For this reason, they provide basic information for making fundamental decisions on accounting policies. One example of such proposals that have come out of the axiomatic system is a proposal to record and report a transaction at the time when it is committed and not at the time when goods or services are received or delivered.[17] This proposal was developed by a minor change in the recognition criteria discussed in the Axiom of Control. Since this proposal is discussed elsewhere, let us consider another proposal in the next section that may be developed out of the axiomatic system discussed above.

INTERCHANGING METHODS IN DEPRECIATION AND IN INVENTORY VALUATION

One of the crucial factors that is built in the three axioms is the allocation of joint costs. This covers not only the joint cost problem in cost accounting, but also the inventory valuation problems, the depreciation problems, and the transfer pricing problems, since they are all concerned with the allocation of costs among periods or divisions. In analyzing the current practices, we find that there are no simple theories that reflect uniformly the ways in which joint costs are allocated.

For example, the purchase cost of merchandise is allocated among the different periods based on a particular adopted inventory valuation method. The purchase cost of buildings, machinery, or equipment is allocated among different periods based on a particular depreciation method. The joint costs in cost accounting are often allocated based on the market values of the merchandise. The transfer prices are often set up based on budgeted or negotiated values. By one method or another, the joint cost problem is solved for each one of these situations in practice. The trouble is that they do not seem to show any uniformity. By reducing the degree of abstraction to the level where individual types of assets are treated differently, we can gain more practicality of the system. Of course, this does not mean that the axiomatic system described above is useless. In fact, as emphasized before, one of

---

[17]See Ijiri [17].

the main contributions of such an approach is to highlight those elements in the accounting practices that are commonly observed, regardless of the types of assets, by separating them from those which are peculiar to each individual asset type. The latter can, of course, be further divided into elements in those practices that are common to all practices concerning a particular asset type and those that are peculiar to a subset of the asset type, and so on.

In this way, we can organize the theories derived from accounting practices into a tree such as given below.

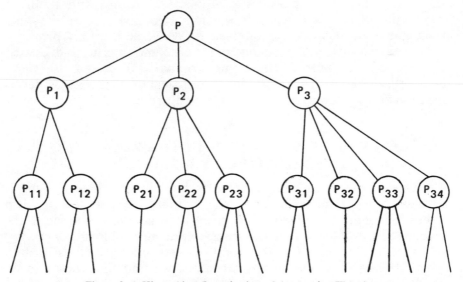

Figure 2. A Hierarchical Organization of Accounting Theories

Here, P represents the set of the three axioms, stated in the most abstract manner. At the next lower level (a less abstractive and more practical level), these axioms are given somewhat more concrete and practical forms for each type of assets. For example, the control criteria discussed in the Axiom of Control are given in a somewhat more specific form for the case of inventories by means of the specifications as to when inventories are considered to be assets of the firm (e.g., when they are shipped from the supplier, when they are received by the firm, or when they are inspected by the firm). It is only after this laborious process of separating essentials from peripherals in the practices that we can say we understand the voluminous accounting practices.

The joint cost problem mentioned above is one of the factors that is left unspecified at the level of axioms. The variety in the manner in which this problem is solved in various parts of accounting provides an interesting issue as to why they are so different from one part to another. Is this because there is something wrong with our process of abstraction? Are they in fact uniformly explainable by a beautiful theory that we have not thought of?

An analogous situation might be the variation of the verb "be" as in I *am*, you *are*, he *is*, etc. These variations bother us if we want to develop grammar, for these differentiations seem to be totally unnecessary, without conveying any additional information. However, this is the reality. No matter how hard scientists try to interpret the phenomena consistently, there always remain some elements of deviations from the rules. The reality is there, no matter how we represent it in rules.

The situations are different, in the case of accounting practices, from the case of ordinary languages as described previously. If we find it desirable to have uniform practices on the joint cost problem, it is possible for us to change them. Let us consider how we might go about doing it and how such a proposal for a change in the practices might be accepted and implemented.

Just as we compared "I *am*" and "you *are*," let us compare the inventory valuation methods and the depreciation methods that are used to solve the joint cost problem. The first question we may ask is, what are the factors peculiar to inventories and fixed assets that require different allocation methods between the two types of assets? An obvious answer is that inventories are likely to turn over within a short period of time, while fixed assets are likely to remain in the firm longer. This seems to be a good enough reason to warrant different treatments. However, let's not give up so easily.

Consider fixed assets whose lives can be measured in terms of the production volumes. Such volumes may be the total volume of products that are expected to be produced from the assets, the total volume of materials that are expected to be processed, or the expected total number of hours of operations, etc. To make the argument more concrete, let us assume that a firm purchases 10 units of air-conditioners of an identical type in April of each year. The life of the air-conditioner is considered to be 3 years, after which the firm trades them in for new ones. The cost of the air-conditioner is $400 per unit and the salvage value $40 per unit. The difference, $360, is normally depreciated in three years under a selected depreciation method in the current practice.

Let us consider this problem from an entirely different angle. The reason the firm buys air-conditioners is not that the firm is interested in owning the machines themselves, but rather that the firm wants to have the service from the machines. In this respect, it is not different from the reason that the firm buys raw materials: the reason the firm buys raw materials is not that they are interested in holding raw materials, but that they want to consume them to obtain the desired services from them. The only difference between the air-conditioners and raw materials from the costing viewpoint is that the total volume of available services is easily measurable in the case of raw materials but not in the case of air-conditioners. Note that the amount of consumption is easily measurable in both cases, if we measure the volume of services of the air-conditioners by, say, the number of hours of operations.

Suppose that we estimate the total service volume of the air-conditioners to be 9,000 hours. Then, a purchase of 10 units of air-conditioners may be recorded in a way analogous to inventory records as a purchase of 90,000 unit-hours of cooling services at the price of 4¢ per unit-hour $\left(\frac{\$400-\$40}{9,000}\right)$. Monthly consumption of the services may then be calculated by multiplying the actual hours of the operations by the unit price.

Now we see exactly the same problem that we encounter in the inventory valuation problem if the unit-hour cost of the air-conditioners varies from year to year. Suppose that, due to inflation, the purchase costs of the air-conditioners have been increased from $400 in 1967 to $500 in 1968 and to $600 in 1969 while the salvage values are also increased from $40 in 1967, $50 in 1968, and $60 in 1969. The unit-hour cost is 4¢, 5¢, and 6¢ for the units purchased in 1967, 1968, and 1969, respectively. Assuming that the firm started purchasing 10 units of the air-conditioners in each year from 1967 and the hours of operations in each year are 3,000 hours for each unit in operation, the entire transactions during the three years may be summarized as follows:

	Purchases			Consumption			Balance		
	Hours	@	Amount	Hours	@	Amount	Hours	@	Amount
1967	90,000	4¢	$3,600				90,000	4¢	$3,600
1967				30,000	4¢	$1,200	60,000	4¢	$2,400
1968	90,000	5¢	$4,500				150,000		
1968				60,000			90,000		
1969	90,000	6¢	$5,400				180,000		
1969				90,000			90,000		

The unit-hour costs and the dollar amounts for consumption and balance in 1968 and 1969 are left open since they depend upon a particular inventory valuation method adopted. Let us calculate them for FIFO, LIFO, and average methods.

	FIFO	LIFO	AVERAGE
1968 Consumption	$2,400	$3,000	$2,760
1968 Balance	$4,500	$3,900	$4,140
1969 Consumption	$4,500	$5,400	$4,770
1969 Balance	$5,400	$3,900	$4,770

It will be easy to see how these numbers are derived. Notice that the amount the firm can charge to expense based on the LIFO method is greater than that under the current practice based on the straight-line depreciation. By introducing the inventory valuation methods into fixed assets, it now becomes possible to take into account the price fluctuation which is not considered in the depreciation methods.

Having explained an application of the inventory valuation methods to fixed assets, let us now consider an application of the depreciation methods to inventories which may be grouped in lots. Suppose, for example, a publisher has printed 5,000 copies of a book at the total cost of $5,000. From this we would immediately figure the unit cost of a copy to be $1 and calculate the value of the inventories and the cost of sales accordingly.

Unfortunately, however, the publisher has no guarantee that they can sell all 5,000 copies printed. The probability that an additional copy will be sold decreases as the number of copies sold increases. In such cases, there is no reason why each copy must be evaluated equally. For example, the sum-of-copy-numbers'-digits method (or the linearly declining balance method) may be applied, and if the publisher has sold 2,000 copies in the first year, the cost of sales may be figured as

$$\$5,000 \times \frac{5,000 + 4,999 + \ldots + 3,001}{1 + 2 + \ldots + 5,000}$$

$$= \$5,000 \times \frac{(5,000 + 3,001) \times 1,000}{(1 + 5,000) \times 2,500}$$

$$= \$5,000 \times \frac{16,002}{25,005} = \$3,200$$

The use of the double-declining balance method is also conceivable, although the computation is more complicated. In the above example, the first copy sold is evaluated at $2, twice the average cost of $1. The "depreciation" rate is then $\frac{2}{5,000} = .0004$ to be applied to the "book value" of the inventories. Thus, the cost of the second copy sold will be $4,998 × .0004 = 1.9992, the cost of the third copy sold will be $4,996 × .0004 = 1.9984, and so on. It will be easy to figure that the book value of the inventories after the sales of 2,000 copies is $\$5,000 \times \left(\frac{4,998}{5,000}\right)^{2,000}$ which is figured to be \$2,247 by using logarithmic computations. Therefore, the cost of sales for the first 2,000 copies is \$2,753, which is less than what the sum-of-copy-numbers'-digits method shows.

In general, these methods are applicable when the economic value per physical unit of inventories decreases (or increases, in which case a decelerated method may be used by reversing the above methods) as more units of inventories are sold or consumed. This aspect has, of course, not been considered in the current accounting practices concerning inventories.

These "interdisciplinary" exchanges of ideas, applying methods developed in one area of accounting to another area, are one of the most important contributions that the axiomatic approach elaborated above can derive. Without once going back to the drawing board to start from scratch, it is often very difficult to break through the traditional habits of thinking which we are so used to because of our experiences in accounting practices.

SANCTIONS AND LEGAL REASONING

Now that we have seen that there is no reason why depreciation methods cannot be applied to inventories and inventory valuation methods cannot be applied to fixed assets, let us consider the implications of this idea in the accounting triad. This is analogous to the situation where we have realized that there is no reason why the verb *are* cannot be used consistently for all types of subjects. What is the value of recognizing the possibility of simplification?

In linguistics, perhaps we cannot do anything. We cannot say that it is wrong usage of English, because this is the way in which English is used. However, in accounting it is possible to change current practices to incorporate these applications if we want to. How then can we go about implementing them in accounting practices? More generally, what is the process by which accounting policies and practices are changed?

Changes in accounting practices are not costless. People are reluctant to change them unless there are some clear benefits from doing so. People will never change to say "I *are*" no matter how hard linguists try to influence them, if there is no benefit to them associated with the change. However, if, for example, leading people in a community started saying "I *are*," then the rest of the community may suddenly see a benefit in changing to say "I *are*" because by doing so they increase the chance of being identified with the leaders of the community, which is a valuable thing for them.

A similar observation may be made in the changes of accounting practices. Accounting practitioners are not interested in changing the practices just to make it easy for accounting theorists to develop theories. Therefore, it is perhaps useless to try to persuade practitioners that they should allow the LIFO method for the depreciation of air-conditioners because it is the most logical thing to do. However, if some firms find it beneficial to use these ideas since they can pay less tax or report higher earnings-per-share, then the likelihood of a change in the practices to incorporate the ideas is substantially increased. If the firm can use the LIFO depreciation method by changing the interpretation of the established accounting policies, then the firm is most likely to do so since they can enjoy the benefit without creating a conflict with the auditors or other enforcement agencies. If, however, the ideas cannot be adopted without changing the existing accounting policies, then they must work through a more complicated legal system.

As we have repeated many times, logic has no direct relationship with the reality of accounting policies and practices. They are there whether they are logical or not. However, as in the above example, if a firm wants to have policies and practices changed, the firm can present the case better when the change is toward making things more logical. The ideas are more likely to be accepted and implemented if they are aimed at making policies and practices more logical.

This is a crucial factor for accounting policy-makers to consider seriously. In order to understand the relationship between logic and sanctions given to accounting policy-makers, let us analyze the nature of accounting sanctions as well as the nature of legal reasoning in some detail.

In any language, the formation rules (to make grammatically correct sentences) and the inference rules (to make true sentences) must be accepted and maintained by people in the society in order for the language to serve them. For this purpose, the society usually maintains some sanctions in enforcing the rules. "Thou shalt not lie" is one of the most common doctrines in any society, because without it the language system of the society breaks down. There are usually explicit penalties attached for those who violate the rule intentionally. Besides, there are often implicit penalties for those who do not conform to the rules even unintentionally.

In accounting, rules are spelled out in the form of generally accepted accounting principles and procedures. These rules are enforced by auditors who are to watch the observance of the rules.

Violations are penalized by means of auditors' qualified opinions, or opinion disclaimed reports. This is true not only in external accounting but also in internal accounting. A firm must have some means by which it can be sure that the rules established for internal accounting are dutifully observed.

In addition to sanctions in enforcing the established rules in accounting language, the sanctions to modify the rules are also explicitly defined. This is a factor that is lacking in ordinary languages. In the latter case, there is no authoritative body who is given the power to change the rules of the language. The changes more or less evolve informally. However, in accounting, there is a formal organizational body, namely the Accounting Principles Board, which is given the power to define and change these rules. The accounting policies established by the Board are aimed at directly influencing the accounting practices.

However, the policies set up by the Board are not necessarily reflected in the accounting practices. This is because their policies, written in the form of opinions, are like any other written laws — they all require interpretation, and interpretation can change over time. Here, the process of legal reasoning interacts with accounting. Let us review the nature of legal reasoning as stated by Levi.

> The basic pattern of legal reasoning is reasoning by example. . . . .It is reasoning from case to case. It is a three-step process described by the doctrine of precedent in which a proposition descriptive of the first case is made into a rule or law and then applied to the next similar situation. The steps are these: similarity is seen between cases; next the rule of law inherent in the first case is announced; then the rule of law is made applicable to the second case. This is a method of reasoning necessary for the law, but it has characteristics which under other circumstances might be considered imperfections. . . . In a sense all reasoning is of this type, . . .but there is an additional requirement which compels the legal process to be this way. Not only do new situations arise, but in addition people's wants change. The categories used in the legal process must be left ambiguous in order to permit the infusion of new ideas. And this is true even where legislation or a constitution is involved. The words used by the legislature or a constitutional convention must come to have new meanings. Furthermore, agreement on any other basis would be impossible. In this manner the laws come to express the ideas of the community and even when written in general terms, in statute or constitution, are molded for the specific case.[18]

When the conformity with the generally accepted accounting principles and procedures becomes a legal issue, it is decided based on

---

[18]E. H. Levi [22, pp. 1-2, 4]. See also C. Morris [27, especially Chapter III].

"reasoning by example." The Accounting Principles Board can specify only a portion of generally accepted accounting principles and procedures.[19] Not only is the rest left entirely to reasoning by example, but also the interpretations of the APB opinions are subject to reasoning by example. This is what is happening in accounting practices even when legal issues are not involved, since people must prepare for such contingencies. Each transaction must, therefore, be judged on its own merit.

"It is not what the prior judge intended that is of any importance; rather it is what the present judge, attempting to see the law as a fairly consistent whole, thinks should be the determining classification."[20] Similarly, Llewellyn states as one of the four canons of legal decisions, "Everything, everything, everything, big or small, a judge may say in an opinion, is to be read with primary reference to the particular dispute, the particular question before him."[21]

What a contrast with an axiomatic system! It appears to be impossible to make any kinds of generalizations. How can we reconcile this fact in the legal system with the logical analysis in accounting theories?

First of all, it must be realized that we are talking about two different areas of accounting with which logic is related. One is the process of building accounting theories and the other is the process of enforcing accounting policies. The logical analysis in accounting theories does not presuppose that accounting practices are logical. Second, even in legal reasoning, the changes in the basic concepts in accounting come very slowly, not to mention any structural changes in accounting.

Third, that the numbers are the basic core of accounting language makes legal reasoning more uniform and generalizable than otherwise, since the numbers demand deductive logic.

The fact that the legal system has such a flexibility must, however, be fully taken into account by accounting policy-makers. This means that the statute of accounting principles and procedures itself can be fairly rigid before making the whole accounting system infeasible to operate. It is perhaps crucial in setting up accounting policies not to adjust here and there in accounting principles and procedures in order to respond to a variety of complaints to the existing accounting practices, but to foresee the need for a structural change in accounting practices that may be required. To provide information for such a decision, an axiomatic approach such as explained earlier

---

[19]See the discussions in P. S. Kemp [20] on the relationship between the APB opinions and the generally accepted accounting principles and procedures.

[20]Levi [22, p. 3].

[21]K. N. Llewellyn [24, p. 42].

and other related logical analyses of accounting practices are essential in highlighting the fundamental elements in accounting practices by separating them from peripheries.

CONCLUSION

In conclusion, we want to emphasize the difference in the roles of accounting theorists and policy-makers. Accounting theorists are scientific observers of accounting practices and their surrounding environment. Their theories are required to have the highest degree of objectivity. The relationship between a theorist and his theory is like the father-son relationship. This is not because the theory is something the theorist has developed with a great care, but rather the theory has and must share a life independent from the theorist. A theory becomes public goods once it is published, regardless of how much affection the theorist has with the theory. A theory may be named after the theorist, such as Newton's law or Einstein's theory, but generally this is done only for the sake of convenience. After all, what is important to the society is what is developed and not who has developed it. A theory that is not completely independent of the theorist does not have an objective value as a theory in the scientific sense of the word. Needless to say, logic plays the central role in making the theory objective.

Contrary to the role of accounting theorists, the role of accounting policy-makers is to define the goals of the accounting profession, evaluate means to achieve the goals, and implement them by establishing accounting policies. Value judgment being a subjective operation, the role of policy-makers is subjective. What they develop is an opinion and not a theory; what it should be and not what it is. When we say Euclid's opinion and Euclid's theory, we are using the term "Euclid's" quite differently; the former to indicate that it is Euclid who had such and such an opinion, and the latter, simply for identification which might as well be replaced by any other name so far as the theory is identified.

As stated before, in reality, a person often plays the role of an accounting theorist, an accounting policy-maker, and an accounting practitioner simultaneously. This is quite confusing especially in research work, because the basic approaches to the problems, required skills to be applied, methods of demonstrating and proving the results, are different in these fields. We must recognize this triad of accounting and clearly identify the role we are playing at each point in time while working in accounting.

The sanctions to establish and enforce accounting policies are a privilege given to the accounting profession. Certainly we should use them with great care. "To be a master" is to take the responsibility of carrying the privilege.

BIBLIOGRAPHY

[1] American Accounting Association. *A Statement of Basic Accounting Theory.* Chicago: American Accounting Association, 1966.

[2] Bedford, N. M. *Income Determination Theory: An Accounting Framework.* Reading, Mass.: Addison-Wesley Publishing Co., Inc., 1965.

[3] Bedford, N. M., and N. Dopuch. "Research Methodology and Accounting Theory — Another Perspective." *The Accounting Review,* Vol. XXXVI, No. 3 (July, 1961), pp. 351–61.

[4] Carnap, R. *The Logical Syntax of Language.* London: Routledge & Kegan Paul, 1937.

[5] ——————. "The Elimination of Metaphysics Through the Logical Analysis of Language," in A. J. Ayer (editor), *Logical Positivism.* New York: Macmillan Co., 1959.

[6] Chambers, R. J. *Accounting, Evaluation and Economic Behavior.* Englewood Cliffs, N. J.: Prentice-Hall, Inc., 1966.

[7] Churchman, C. W. *Prediction and Optimal Decision.* Englewood Cliffs, N. J.: Prentice-Hall, Inc., 1961.

[8] Deinzer, H. T. *Development of Accounting Thought.* New York: Holt, Rinehart and Winston, Inc., 1965.

[9] Devine, C. T. *Essays in Accounting Theory.* Berkeley, California: C. T. Devine, 1962.

[10] Dopuch, N. "Metaphysics of Pragmatism and Accountancy." *The Accounting Review,* Vol. XXXVII, No. 2 (April, 1962), pp. 251–62.

[11] Edwards, E. O., and P. W. Bell. *The Theory and Measurement of Business Income.* Berkeley, Calif: University of California Press, 1961.

[12] Gardner, M. *Mathematical Puzzles and Diversions.* New York: Simon and Schuster, 1961.

[13] Grady, P. *Inventory of Generally Accepted Accounting Principles for Business Enterprises.* New York: American Institute of Certified Public Accountants, 1965.

[14] Hendriksen, E. S. *Accounting Theory.* Homewood, Illinois: Richard D. Irwin, Inc., 1965.

[15] Ijiri, Y. "Axioms and Structures of Conventional Accounting Measurement." *The Accounting Review,* Vol. XL, No. 1 (January, 1965), pp. 36–53.

[16] ——————. *The Foundations of Accounting Measurement: A Mathematical, Economic, and Behavioral Inquiry.* Englewood Cliffs, N. J.: Prentice-Hall, Inc., 1967.

[17] ——————. "On the Commitment Basis of Recording and Reporting Transactions." Working Paper, Carnegie-Mellon University, January, 1969.

[18] Ijiri, Y., and R. K. Jaedicke. "Reliability and Objectivity of Accounting Measurements." *The Accounting Review*, Vol. XLI, No. 3 (July, 1966), pp. 474–83.

[19] Katz, J. J. *The Philosophy of Language*. New York: Harper and Row, 1966.

[20] Kemp, P. S. "The Authority of the Accounting Principles Board." *The Accounting Review*, Vol. XL, No. 4 (October, 1965), pp. 782–87.

[21] Kleene, S. C. *Mathematical Logic*. New York: John Wiley & Sons, Inc., 1967.

[22] Levi, E. H. *An Introduction to Legal Reasoning*. Chicago: University of Chicago Press, 1949.

[23] Littleton, A. C. *Structure of Accounting Theory*. Chicago: American Accounting Association, 1953.

[24] Llewellyn, K. N. *The Bramble Bush: On Our Law and Its Study*. Dobbs Ferry, New York: Oceana Publications, Inc., 1960.

[25] Mattessich, R. *Accounting and Analytical Methods*. Homewood, Ill.: Richard D. Irwin, Inc., 1964.

[26] Moonitz, M. *The Basic Postulates of Accounting*. New York: American Institute of Certified Public Accountants, 1961.

[27] Morris, C. *How Lawyers Think*. Cambridge, Mass.: Harvard University Press, 1937.

[28] Paton, W. A., and A. C. Littleton. *An Introduction to Corporate Accounting Standards*. Chicago: American Accounting Association, 1940.

[29] Sprouse, R. T., and M. Moonitz. *A Tentative Set of Broad Accounting Principles for Business Enterprises*. New York: American Institute of Certified Public Accountants, 1962.

[30] Vatter, W. J. *The Fund Theory of Accounting and Its Implications for Financial Reports*. Chicago: University of Chicago Press, 1947.

[31] Wittgenstein, L. *Philosophical Investigations*. (Translated in English by G. E. M. Anscombe) Oxford: Basil Blackwell, 1953.

LOGIC AND SANCTIONS IN ACCOUNTING
CRITIQUE

Claude S. Colantoni*

Mathematics, as an instrument for computing, has played an important role in the social sciences. However, this "practical" application of mathematics has often served to obscure its potential use in a more creative capacity. A modern view of mathematics recognizes not merely its application as a calculating device, but its use as a language in which complex theories may be expressed precisely. In addition to the clarity of exposition which is achieved through its use, mathematics is equipped with powerful analytical tools for theory development, including logical rules which govern the validity of the deductive process. The major contribution of Ijiri's paper has been to demonstrate the potential value of the use of mathematics as a logical language in solving problems in accounting theory. Several significant avenues of research which have been opened by Ijiri will be discussed below with some suggested extensions of the ideas which he presented.

MATHEMATICS, LOGIC, AND ACCOUNTING

In recent years social scientists have become increasingly aware of the need for precision in their work. This awareness often results from a recognition that "natural language" formulations of a problem introduce ambiguities and complexities which prevent the scientist from defining the problem. Consequently, to eliminate linguistic impurities, many social scientists have begun employing mathematics as the primary language in which theories, problems, and solutions may be expressed.

For example, the history of the concept of utility in economic theory is filled with many highly ambiguous theories of value. Controversy existed for centuries concerning the notions of "value in use" versus "value in exchange," and "cardinal" versus "ordinal" utility.

*The author would like to express appreciation to Charles A. Tritschler for his many helpful comments and suggestions.

29

A major problem arose concerning the existence of utility functions, but because of a highly ambiguous concept of value, the formulation was not precise enough to admit a solution. It was not until recent years that a mathematical statement of the problem was given and a rigorous analysis applied. Furthermore, all modern theories of utility now extensively use mathematical theories from analysis and topology.

In his fourth section, "Logical Analyses in Accounting," Professor Ijiri has suggested a similar use of mathematics in accounting. When discussing the difficulty which might be associated with constructing a unifying theory for both inventory valuation and depreciation methods he states:

> Here, the set theory can be very helpful in breaking away our conceptual boundaries. Instead of considering each type of asset separately, we try to represent all assets by a set of points (or by a set of sets if necessary). In associating assets with points on a sheet of paper, we often find that our concept of assets is ambiguous. (p. 14).

In section five, "Interchanging Methods In Depreciation and In Inventory Valuation," this idea is explored at some length with highly satisfying results. Ijiri has used mathematics as a tool for abstracting theories of depreciation and inventory valuation (as opposed to its use as a tool for *calculating* depreciation or the value of inventory) and demonstrated the similarities in the two seemingly unrelated accounting processes. For instance, it can no longer be taken for granted that the methods of FIFO and LIFO are inappropriate for use in depreciating physical assets or that the list of acceptable inventory valuation methods for a book publisher does not include "sum-of-copy-numbers'-digits method." As with the theory of value in economics, the problem concerning the appropriateness of depreciation methods or inventory valuation techniques has now been stated more precisely and (at least potentially) a solution given. Many other ambiguous and ill-defined concepts in accounting require a precise statement. Certainly not all problems can be easily reduced to mathematical statements. But one necessary avenue of future research will be directed toward finding precise formulations of those controversial issues in accounting which can be stated in the language of mathematics.

Mathematics, of course, is also a language of special power, since embedded within it is a capability for rigorous logical analysis. Many of the achievements of social scientists can be directly related to their ability to reason carefully; to think logically. Often failures can be traced to an inability to properly apply rules of valid inference.

A major contribution of Ijiri's paper has been to illustrate how fundamental concepts and practices in accounting can be logically constructed. For example, in his section "Logical Analyses in Accounting," Ijiri presents an axiomatic system and the corresponding inference rules for the conventional accounting valuation based on historical cost. With this set of axioms and rules Ijiri has demonstrated in previous works how much of financial accounting follows logically.[1]

Of course, the necessity of employing such rigorous analysis might be challenged. However, as Ijiri points out on page 9, "The practices in accounting are not always logically set up." He also adds on page 23, "As we have repeated many times, logic has no direct relationship with the reality of accounting policies and practices. They are there whether they are logical or not." Other accountants might disclaim any need for being logical; that it is an impractical academic exercise. However, any science must be constructed from certain basic principles in a consistent manner, and it is the apparatus of logical deduction and inference which makes this possible. The rules of deductive logic are preventive medicine to the scientist in keeping him from saying too much, too fast; to prevent him from arriving at invalid conclusions or generating inconsistent theories. Most accountants are already aware of the perils of asserting conclusions which are invalid. But how carefully have accountants considered the difficulties associated with inconsistent theories and practices?

Consistency of a theory (i.e., the absence of a proposition and its negation in the theory) is of paramount importance. Consider the following statements in this regard.

> Inconsistency in a system renders it virtually useless for a particular discipline, since any *conclusion* may be derived from the system by a certain sequence of operations; existence of such a sequence is implied by the logical theorem.[2]

And,

> Experience has shown however, that a much more fundamental and critical question is, does the system imply any contradictory theorem? If it does, clearly something is wrong and it is useless to inquire into other questions until this defect has been eliminated.[3]

Despite these menacing warnings, one observes accountants using both FIFO and LIFO methods for inventory valuation, as well as the

---

[1]Yuji Ijiri [4 and 6].
[2]Thomas H. Williams and Charles H. Griffin [12, p. 36].
[3]Raymond J. Wilder [11, p. 23].

lower-of-cost-or-market method. It seems to me to be an open question as to whether the accepted accounting principles as they now stand are intended to be consistent *with one another*. But the fact that certain inconsistencies may exist in presently accepted accounting practice in no way alters our conclusion. Any theory must be internally consistent if it is to be of value, and therefore a formal approach to accounting theory and practice is necessary.

ACCOUNTING THEORY

Some of the more detailed points will now be discussed with some possible modifications and extensions to the theory presented in the paper. On page 4, Professor Ijiri states, "It is clear that accounting practices are the basic objects of studies for formulating accounting theories and policies." He then goes on to present, "The Triad of Accounting Theories, Policies, and Practices." In an important sense, "The Triad" should be expanded to include relevant subject matter and methodology from other disciplines. Many problems in accounting today might have solutions, or at least be better understood, if the progress made in economics, mathematics, psychology, and engineering were adopted by accountants. For example, the problem of price level adjustment in financial statements was the topic of one paper delivered at this conference. By looking to accounting theory one only sees a practice of not adjusting statements. However, by considering modern theories in economics and finance, one can find a strong theoretical basis for preparing price level adjusted statements. After all, the problem of "real" value has been a subject of study by economists for centuries. As mentioned earlier, it has even achieved a status of great mathematical and theoretical sophistication. Consequently, a strong theory to support a practice of price level adjustments is available in subject areas closely related to accounting. Clearly, examples like this could be drawn from many different areas. While his own accounting logic does not contemplate price level adjustments, I hasten to add that Ijiri *does not* overlook the advantages which accrue from interdisciplinary work. The subject matter of the paper alone illustrates the advantages of employing logic in accounting. Hence the paper is, in itself, interdisciplinary in nature. However, a more explicit incorporation of interdisciplinary investigations in "The Triad" would seem desirable.

A further comment on the "Triad" concerns the following statement by Ijiri:

> The corresponding theory-building process in accounting will then be seen as a process of abstracting from a mass of observations of accounting practices without arguing whether or not they ought to be different from what they are. (p. 5).

This of course, represents a strong empirical orientation for the theorists. As expressed by E. Bright Wilson:

> When a hypothesis has been devised to fit the observed facts, it becomes possible to apply the rules of logic and deduce various consequences. Logic does not enter science until this stage is reached.[4]

However, it is also productive for the theorist in the social sciences to think of what could or should be. This latter type of theory building is most often described by the term "normative." In comparing the difference, one might say that an empirical theory is built upon "what is" while a normative theory is built upon a belief about "what should be." In a science like accounting, where alteration of existing practice is possible, normative theories should be of primary importance. For instance, a normative orientation to the problem of what information should be reported by accountants would result in reports which would more closely satisfy the needs of the users of accounting data. Ijiri recognizes the normative aspects of accounting, but he suggests that it is the policy makers, and not the theorists, who make these judgments. In fact, Ijiri points out that, ". . . in reality, a person often plays the role of an accounting theorist, an accounting policy-maker, and an accounting practitioner simultaneously." (p. 26). However, many important policy considerations arise only after a theorist has proffered some normative theory, and explored its consequences.

On page 6 Professor Ijiri compares accounting with linguistics. In addition to the valuable discussion presented in the paper, certain additional points might be stressed. Accountants are predominantly concerned with descriptions of real objects (surrogates as described by Ijiri in earlier works [6, 8]) rather than the objects themselves. For any accounting object there are an infinite number of characteristics which can be measured. Any finite number of characteristics can serve as the basis for a partial description of an object. That is, if a finite number of precise measurements were taken of the object, then the object can be considered as partially described. As the number of characteristics measured is increased, more becomes "known" about the object's underlying reality. As more measurements are taken, a better approximation of the complete description of that object can be found. Thus, the issue concerning valuation measures (descriptions)

---

[4]E. Bright Wilson, Jr. [13, p. 27].

should be directed toward finding that alternative method which yields the best approximation of the *actual economic state;* the one which reveals the most about some underlying economic reality of the firm, as well as providing a measure for "who won the game." In this regard I find the declining balance method for inventory valuation delightful since it may well serve to describe the underlying physical process in some circumstances more validly than other procedures.

Also, if descriptions of objects are intended to "represent" objects, the policy making authority permitted the Accounting Principles Board should be so oriented. That is, the policies established should represent attempts at trying to make accounting reports more closely conform with the underlying reality described. For example, the appropriateness of FIFO and LIFO should be governed by whether an approximate description of the *actual economic flow* results from the use of the technique.

An even more complex issue concerning descriptions is also involved here. All measurement and description takes place in the midst of imperfect knowledge. It is therefore desirable to identify with a report (description) the uncertainty associated with it. For example, when inventories are counted some error (or inaccuracy) is inevitable, and information about the uncertainty (statistical error) associated with the reported value is desirable. Some investigations into this question have been made, including the development of a theory of accounting description.[5] The area of uncertainty and description still remains as an important area of inquiry for accountants in the future.

Finally, I would like to comment on Ijiri's axiom system developed in his section entitled "Logical Analyses in Accounting." Every science is built upon a base of certain assumed truths (axioms). The axioms cannot be in contradiction with observed facts. However, it may not be possible to demonstrate the truth of the postulates. It seems desirable therefore, that axioms be constructed at the "grass roots level," as close to the intended foundations as possible. For example, in the economics of Marshall, demand functions were postulated, while in modern economic theory axioms characterize preference orderings, which in turn yield as deductive consequences demand functions. In this manner one has distinct advantages of uncovering the conditions which are necessary and sufficient for the existence of demand functions (if one assumes the existence of preference orderings).

In this spirit I suggest that in place of the "Axiom of Quantities" one begin with axioms concerning empirical relations among objects

---

[5]Claude S. Colantoni [1] and Charles E. Gearing [3].

and empirical operations on objects, and derive necessary and sufficient conditions for the existence of quantities. By doing this one not only discovers more concerning the nature of accounting quantities, but in implementing the theory the isomorphic relationship between the theory and the real world application can be more fundamentally established. Ijiri has already made significant contributions to the theory of accounting measurement. However, the research question concerning the conditions under which quantity measures do exist, and their relationship to value measures, still remains unsolved.

Also, the "Axiom of Exchange" as postulated by Ijiri abstracts away the problem of the allocation of costs. This, of course, from a theoretical point of view cannot be criticized. However, by starting from a more fundamental point one may be able to derive as a consequence a solution to this knotty issue of cost allocation, or at least a conditional solution based upon certain assumptions. Therefore, although the axiom system postulated by Ijiri represents a significant contribution to accounting theory, more research is possible and necessary before it can be commonly accepted.

SOME IMPLICATIONS

First, with regard to commonly accepted methodology, Ijiri has suggested a need for more explicit incorporation of the tools of logic in accounting research. Through the use of logic, closer adherence to the norms of valid reasoning can be achieved. Of course, the use of logic as a methodological tool often necessitates abstract problem definition using the language of mathematics. However, the use of mathematics reduces the ambiguities caused by the "natural language" and renders questions more amenable to rigorous analysis. Once these advantages have been recognized by accountants, logic and mathematics will become standard tools in the methodology of accounting research.

As a consequence of the use of mathematics in accounting, a second implication will be the evolution of a field of research called "mathematical accounting." Similar in nature to mathematical economics, research in mathematical accounting would be concerned with the application of modern mathematical tools to problems in accounting theory. In addition to the advantages which will directly result from the use of mathematics in accounting, some desirable secondary effects will occur. The interdisciplinary nature of mathematical accounting can provide accountants with a natural link to the related fields of mathematical economics, management science, and mathematical psychology. The recent progress in these related fields will then be made more accessible to the accounting profession.

Further, the use of more mathematics in accounting research will encourage more students of accounting to become acquainted with advanced mathematics (beyond calculus and linear algebra). Courses in mathematics and statistics might even be introduced into a student's program at the expense of some accounting courses. Such a change would have two effects. One, the students produced would be methodologically capable of approaching accounting problems from a more rigorous and abstract point of view. Also, the students, by removing some required courses in accounting, would become less inundated with existing methods and theories, thereby motivating them to explore new approaches to the problems in accounting.

In final defense of a theoretical approach to problems in accounting, let me close with a statement from Alfred Tarski:

> . . . it is inimical to the progress of science to measure the importance of any research exclusively or chiefly in terms of its usefulness and applicability. We know from the history of science that many important results and discoveries have had to wait centuries before they were applied in any field . . . It may be unpopular and out-of-date to say — but I do not think that a scientific result which gives us a better understanding of the world and makes it more harmonious in our eyes should be held in lower esteem than, say, an invention which reduces the cost of paving roads, or improves household plumbing.[6]

BIBLIOGRAPHY

[1] Colantoni, Claude S. "The Use of Mathematical Structures in Describing, Measuring, and Reporting the State of a Firm Under Conditions of Uncertainty." Unpublished Ph.D. dissertation, Purdue University, Lafayette, Indiana, 1968.

[2] Curry, Haskell B. *Foundations of Mathematical Logic.* New York: McGraw-Hill, Inc., 1963.

[3] Gearing, Charles E. "A Dynamic Model of the Firm Under Risk Based Upon the Concept of a Stochastic Commodity." Unpublished Ph.D. dissertation, Purdue University, Lafayette, Indiana, 1966.

[4] Ijiri, Yuji. "Axioms and Structures of Conventional Accounting Measurement." *The Accounting Review,* Vol. XL, No. 1 (January, 1965), pp. 36–53.

[5] Ijiri, Yuji. "Physical Measures and Multi-Dimensional Accounting." *Research in Accounting Measurement,* edited by Robert K. Jaedicke, Yuji Ijiri, and Oswald Nielsen. New York: American Accounting Association, 1966.

---

[6]Alfred Tarski [10, pp. 41-2].

[6] Ijiri, Yuji. *The Foundations of Accounting Measurement.* Englewood Cliffs, New Jersey: Prentice Hall, 1967.

[7] Ijiri, Yuji. "Logic and Sanctions in Accounting." Paper presented at Accounting Colloquium I. The University of Kansas, Lawrence, Kansas. April 24–26, 1969.

[8] Ijiri, Yuji, Robert K. Jaedicke, and Kenneth E. Knight. "The Effects of Accounting Alternatives on Management Decisions." *Research in Accounting Measurement,* edited by Robert K. Jaedicke, Yuji Ijiri, and Oswald Nielsen. New York: American Accounting Association, 1966.

[9] Jaedicke, Robert K., Yuji Ijiri, and Oswald Nielsen (editors). *Research in Accounting Measurement.* New York: American Accounting Association, 1966.

[10] Tarski, Alfred. "The Semantic Conception of Truth." Leonard Linsky (editor). *Semantics and the Philosophy of Language.* Urbana, Illinois: The University of Illinois Press, 1952. Pp. 13–47.

[11] Wilder, Raymond L. *The Foundations of Mathematics.* New York: John Wiley & Sons, Inc., 1952.

[12] Williams, Thomas H., and Charles H. Griffin. *The Mathematical Dimension of Accountancy.* Cincinnati, Ohio: South-Western Publishing Co., 1964.

[13] Wilson, E. Bright, Jr. *An Introduction to Scientific Research.* New York: McGraw-Hill, Inc., 1952.

CRITIQUE
Robert E. Jensen

SCIENCE AND ACCOUNTING THEORY

My remarks will be prefaced by a few comments regarding universal accounting theory. At present there is no universal system of accounting theory, nor will there likely be such a system during our lifetime. Accounting is a part of the respective information environments of various decision makers. Diversity among the types of decisions that must be made, complicated and unknown goal hierarchies, changing technological constraints on information systems, lack of understanding of how decisions are or should be reached, and interacting decisions, make the entire field of accounting far too difficult to build on a simple structure of underlying principles. It would seem that a universal structure of accounting theory cannot precede a universal system of decision theory. Our limited knowledge and imperfect understanding of decision problems prevent us from identifying common elements or basic principles underlying accounting measurements to be provided for such general, vague problems.

Professor Ijiri briefly discusses accounting theory in terms of a process from which accounting theory may be created. On page 5 he states:

> The corresponding theory-building process in accounting will then be seen as a process of abstracting from a mass of observations of accounting practices without arguing whether or not they ought to be different from what they are. We accept them as they are and try to develop theories which will describe a maximum volume of observations by the simplest set of concepts....

This statement relates to the common view of the theory-building process in physical and biological sciences having the goal of observing and explaining phenomena of nature. Many facts are observed and hypotheses are tested, followed by attempts to identify common elements which relate known facts. Unlike physical and biological scientists, accounting theorists do not have a foundation of several millenia of scientific observation and measurement of

38

relevant phenomena. For Professor Ijiri the modest set of facts under study are certain accounting practices which have evolved in commercial activity. His objective is to identify the common elements of these practices and relate them to one another in a systematic manner. Although this approach is far from unique in accounting study, he has managed to construct an axiomatic system of valuation rules which is much more basic and concise than those developed by many other accounting scholars. It must be recognized, however, that these elements are common to only a subset of diverse modern-day accounting practices.

Professor Ijiri discusses his approach in relation to ordinary language philosophy and logical empiricism. (p. 6). The analogy here is quite interesting, for we observe that many proposed systems of accounting tend to conform to the "top-down" approach of logical empiricism, resulting in highly logical accounting structures, e.g., — those of Sprouse and Moonitz,[1] Edwards and Bell,[2] Chambers,[3] and earlier writers. These accounting theories are attacked as impractical because elements of the theories are stated in economic terms of "what should be" or "what should be if" rather than "what is." Many practitioners are apparently unwilling to accept some of the assumptions or premises implicit in economic logic extended to accounting theory.

Criticism has been leveled by others at economic theories themselves which are "top down" in the sense that "economic man," "perfect competition," and other premises are artificial constructs that do not exist in reality. Recent social science literature is replete with behavioral criticisms of traditional economic theory. Certainly there is a need for economic theories founded on grass roots observations of individual and social human behavior. But this does not imply that the "top down" approach must at the same time be abandoned or that accounting theorists should stop seeking parallels between science and accounting. I am reminded of a statement from Von Neumann and Morgenstern, who refer to mathematical procedures in theoretical physics as they relate to formation of economic theory:

> At this point it is appropriate to mention another familiar argument of economic literature which may be revived as an objection against the mathematical procedure.
>
> In order to elucidate the conceptions we are applying to economics, we have given and may give again some illustrations from physics. There are many social scientists who object to the drawing of such parallels on various grounds, among which

[1]Robert T. Sprouse and Maurice Moonitz [10].
[2]Edgar O. Edwards and Philip W. Bell [4].
[3]Raymond J. Chambers [2].

is generally found the assertion that economic theory cannot be modeled after physics since it is a science of social, of human phenomena, has to take psychology into account, etc. Such statements are at least premature. It is without doubt reasonable to discover what has led to progress in other sciences, and to investigate whether the application of the same principles may not lead to progress in economics also. Should the need for application of different principles arise, it could be revealed only in the course of the actual development of economic theory.[4]

Professor Ijiri's approach in this paper and in his earlier book [5] is interesting in that he views accounting practice as it is rather than as it "ought to be" in terms of economic reasoning. Attempts should be made to go even further than Ijiri has gone, i.e., I would prefer to view the theory-building process in accounting as a process of observing masses of scientific observations from decision environments and thought processes of managers, investors, and government officials. Perhaps there are common elements that can be related to the common elements of certain existing or proposed accounting processes. Only then can theorists effectively guide policy formulation in accounting on the basis of evidence of systematic, scientific observations which are relevant. Until that time, policy formation will have to rest on the personal experiences and observations of persons selectively chosen to subjectively "judge" what alternative accounting policies are to be adopted.

Referring to the hierarchy of the degrees of generality suggested by Katz as an approach lying between "top down" logical empiricism and grass roots ordinary language philosophy in linguistics, Ijiri (p. 9) proposes that the same approach might be useful in constructing accounting theories from accounting practices. I would go further and extend this approach to constructing accounting theories from decision behavior studies. Accounting, we would agree, is intended to "serve" decision makers. Accordingly, "local rules" must differ in serving decision makers along a continuum between economic man and the Burmese businessman who, according to Miller and Starr, prefers the pleasure of bargaining to the achievement of profit.[5]

The objective is to establish degrees of generality of decision rules and to relate these rules with accounting processes designed to serve a continuum of decision makers. In this manner we can better establish a hierarchy of the degrees of generality of accounting rules. Beyond existing accounting practices, we need

---

[4]John Von Neumann and Oskar Morgenstern [11, pp. 3–4].
[5]D. W. Miller and M. K. Starr [8, p. 3].

to discover how accounting information is and can be used in economic decision making. For example, suppose it was discovered that the output of current accounting practices is largely ignored by most decision makers; then efforts to develop only theories of current accounting practices would seem shortsighted.

Professor Ijiri possibly allows for a more general outlook in his conclusion where he states: "Accounting theorists are scientific observers of accounting practices and their surrounding environment." (p. 26).

The "surrounding environment" appears to me to be a richer area of grass roots study than practices alone. At the same time the less tedious role of a logical empiricist in accounting study is not obsolete, for desirable innovations in accounting processes may arise from both approaches to the construction of a theoretical framework. Some writers have a less optimistic outlook:

> Accounting might seem to be scientific in point of view since it deals in some measure with objectively determined facts. Accounting, however, can never become completely scientific, because its factual materials can never be determined with complete and conclusive objectivity. Business does not lend itself to laboratory analysis and its activities do not follow mathematical formulae.[6]

Certainly there are many unanswered problems in applying the scientific approaches of the physical and biological sciences to the behavioral sciences. Perhaps we ultimately must await a revolutionary approach in behavioral science research in order to develop a universal system of accounting theory, or better yet, a universal system of decision information theory.

The problem here is aptly noted by Churchman:

> The empirical investigation of what men really want is possible only if men are educated as well as possible concerning the outcomes of policies, and only if men are free to choose. Evidence of man's true values is to be found in his spoken words, or his consumer practices, or his voting behavior only if he is free of ignorance and other constraints. Hence the extreme difficulty in the empirical determination of values, and hence the inevitable conclusion that today we do not know even in a very rough form what the human animal wants.[7]

A tremendous dilemma exists for which we have no answer. Accounting is designed to serve without knowing the wants and needs of those

---

[6]W. A. Paton and A. C. Littleton [9, p. 19].
[7]C. W. Churchman [3, p. vii].

it is to serve. At the same time, what accountants provide to those they serve still leaves them in varying degrees of ignorance so that they are not really free to choose among alternatives.

SOME COMMENTS ON PROFESSOR IJIRI'S RESEARCH METHODOLOGY

Theories are to be constructed out of facts. We might observe that the source for Professor Ijiri's facts for his axiomatic system seems to me to be arbitrarily chosen hypothetical journal entries conforming to bookkeeping rules and illustrations found in accounting textbooks, although this source is ambiguous in his statements on this matter. On page 13 he says:

> How were the axioms and valuation rules derived? They were derived by observing a large volume of journal entries and by trying to reduce them into a small set of categories.

Professor Ijiri suggests that his research methodology is akin to that of an ordinary language philosopher in the sense that his facts drawn from "accounting practice" are analogous to the facts of a language philosopher drawn from unstructured natural languages. It is interesting to compare a quotation from Katz with a quotation from Ijiri in this regard. Katz at one point states:

> The self-defeating assumption, which went wholly unchallenged within each of these movements [logical empiricism and ordinary language philosophy], was that natural languages are highly unstructured and unsystematic conglomerations of verbal constructions. Thus, fluency is thought of as a habit or disposition to respond verbally to situations of the appropriate sort, with particular verbal constructions elicited as responses being under only very weak linguistic constraints due to the unstructured and unsystematic character of language.[8]

Compare the above comment with a previous quotation from Ijiri [5, p. 88]:

> Unfortunately, conventional accounting is a collection of many different principles and practices, which, in some cases, are mutually inconsistent. Hence, no systematic theories can describe them all.

It seems to me that Professor Ijiri has assumed *a priori* that conventional accounting practices are unstructured and unsystematic. Hence, he arbitrarily chose to systematize only a small

---

[8]J. J. Katz [7, p. 16].

subset of practices which are already recognized to be the most structured and systematic processes in accounting. Furthermore, his observations were not based on actual practices but textbook descriptions, which by their very nature are already abstractions of reality. The analogy here would be a case where an ordinary language philosopher observes only scholarly works of a single language or some highly systematized portion of a single language. This is not, however, the viewpoint of the true ordinary language philosopher.

THE AXIOMATIC STRUCTURE OF HISTORICAL COST VALUATION

RELATION TO EARLIER STUDIES

Professor Ijiri's concepts of "asset classes," "quantities," and "exchanges" have been identified by others under identical or related terms, notably Paton and Littleton. For example, consider the following quotation:

> In general, the only definite facts available to represent exchange transactions objectively and to express them homogeneously are the price-aggregates involved in the exchanges; hence such data constitute the basic subject matter of accounting.
> Since specific costs express significant parts of the total effort expended in producing and selling a commodity or service, they may be assembled by operating divisions, product parts, or time intervals as if they had the power, like their physical counterparts, of cohering in groups.[9]

In this statement we see a correspondence between "cohering in groups" and Ijiri's concept of quantities, and "exchange transactions" and Ijiri's concept of exchanges.

Value Allocation and Imputation Rules given by Ijiri are a formal statement of the "costs attach" argument of Paton and Littleton [9, pp. 13–14]:

> . . . it is a basic concept of accounting that costs can be marshaled into new groups that possess real significance. It is as if costs had a power of cohesion when properly brought into contact.
> It is not necessary to assume a cost theory of value in order to explain the concept that costs cohere. Costs are not marshaled to show value or worth. In their new position they are still costs,

---

[9]Paton and Littleton [9, p. 7].

that is, price-aggregates of exchange transactions; they have merely been regrouped.

Similarly the concept of "basic class" and the Value Comparison Rule are grounded in the realization concept [9, p. 49]:

> Earning must not be confused with realization. Revenue is realized, according to the dominant view, when it is evidenced by cash receipts or receivables, or other new liquid assets. Implicit here are two tests: (1) conversion through legal sale or similar process; (2) validation through the acquisition of liquid assets.

SPECIAL FEATURES OF THE AXIOMATIC STRUCTURE OF HISTORICAL COST VALUATION

Many writers have described the historical cost basis of valuation along the same lines as Paton and Littleton, particularly textbooks of accounting, old and new. There are, however, a number of features which set Ijiri's recent axiomatic structure of such a system apart from earlier contributions and restatements. One feature is that Ijiri avoids making any reference to arguments for or against such a system, e.g., he does not mention traditional "objective evidence" arguments for and "lack of comparability" arguments against adherence to historical cost. He seeks only to present a logically consistent framework for the process itself.

By using general set theoretic concepts such as entities, sets, classes, ordered pairs, and measure functions, he avoids bringing to the system many concepts having preconceived meanings. For example, the term "basic class" has no special meaning other than to assume it exists apart from "nonbasic classes," whereas the term "liquid assets" typically used in other writings requires a more specific definition and further elaboration, so the definition of "liquidity" becomes necessary.

Professor Ijiri's system is not the first attempt to translate elements of accounting practice into set theory and logic. Winborne [12] wrote a Ph.D. dissertation entitled *The Application of Sets and Symbolic Logic to Selected Accounting Principles and Practices.* Dr. Winborne's system is more extensive in the sense that it deals with periodicity, depreciation, equity transactions, and other accounting concepts in terms of the calculus of propositions. However, from my viewpoint, the approach taken by Winborne is less useful. Her attempt seems to be merely an unstructured translation of some verbal descriptions of accounting into symbolic relations without any subsequent mathematical analysis. The result is a collection of unsystematized elements having doubtful relevance in accounting theory, although there might be some usefulness in such an approach in teaching accounting.

Professor Ijiri, on the other hand, presents a more systematized approach with a set of axioms necessary to support a set of historical cost valuation rules. His analysis serves to focus attention on basic elements rather than peripheral issues and interpretations. It may be concisely stated in mathematical form.

LIMITATIONS OF THE AXIOMATIC STRUCTURE OF HISTORICAL COST VALUATION

Professor Ijiri's axiomatic system has some serious limitations, many of which are noted by Professor Ijiri [5, pp. 98-99] himself in various parts of his earlier book.

There are some other limitations, however, which seem to me to be implicit in his analysis. For example, are the three axioms alone sufficient to support the valuation rules? The Value Allocation Rule explicitly assumes that a "value" is assigned to every resource class of a firm in basic class quantity units — dollars if the basic class represents cash or its equivalent. In exchanges, these values are assigned by the Value Imputation Rule. However, initially it must be assumed that the only non-empty resource class is the basic class or some other axiom is required concerning basic-class value imputation of non-basic resource classes prior to exchanges within these classes. In an earlier discussion, Professor Ijiri [5, p. 98] attempts to circumvent this problem by excluding from feasibility any initial proprietary investment of resources not in the basic class. However, my question concerns whether this assumption must be formalized in the axioms themselves in order to claim that the axioms are *necessary and sufficient* to support the valuation rules. This is all that I will mention on this particular issue.

Professor Ijiri contends (p. 16) that his three axioms are sufficient to describe "a majority of accounting practices on journal entries and asset valuation." After a careful look at his axiomatic system, I have some doubts as to whether the majority of various accounting practices do in fact "fit" his system in terms of my own subjective appraisal of what constitutes "majority" in this case.

For example, the Value Allocation Rule bases all allocations of costs according to a direct proportion of decrement quantity measure to total resource class quantity measure. But even the most vocal advocates of historical costing do not limit historical costing to such a restricted allocation basis:

> Even in the handling of direct material charges, for example,
> it is often necessary to recognize that the problem of assignment

> is a matter of economic rather than of physical flow. Thus the entire cost of a sheet of leather consumed in making shoes is charged to the product notwithstanding the fact that a considerable portion of the sheet becomes waste material.[10]

Since we do not have a large body of scientific observations concerning actual accounting practices, we have no way of knowing to what extent such economic considerations override quantity proportions in cost allocations.

Next consider all period expenses which are not capitalized by an accounting system (administrative, selling, and distribution expenses). For convenience we assume that these are all paid in terms of decrement to the basic class (cash). Since these expenses are not capitalized, the resource class to which they all correspond could be viewed as the empty (null) set. According to the Value Imputation Rule, the value of such a non-basic resource class would be increased by the value of the basic decrement (the cash amount of the expenses). But this contradicts Basic Valuation Rule 2 which states that the value of an empty class must always be zero. Hence, it seems to me that traditional accounting treatment of all such expenses lies outside Professor Ijiri's valuation system.

Now consider material, labor, and overhead costs in a manufacturing operation producing multiple classes of inventory quantities. Possible examples of such processes are petroleum refineries, automobile assembly lines, and shoe manufacturing. In such instances, overhead is a joint cost and in addition, material and labor are typically joint costs among two or more non-fungible classes of product. My own experiences would indicate that joint costs on this level are more common than not in manufacturing processes. But a serious weakness in Professor Ijiri's system of valuation rules is the inability to handle joint costs in situations where resource increments in an exchange belong to more than one resource class. Also, standard costing rather than historical costing is employed by many manufacturing firms. Hence I suspect that Ijiri's system might not necessarily apply in the "majority" of manufacturing processes, or, for that matter, even in cases where material and labor may be applied according to a variety of application rates not covered in this system.

On the other hand, it is quite common in many merchandising firms to depart from historical costing, because the lower-of-cost-or-market and retail methods of valuation are extremely common. Departures from historical cost are obviously not covered by Professor Ijiri's historical cost valuation rules. Hence, we cannot necessarily

[10]Paton and Littleton [9, p. 71].

assume that inventory costs can be handled by his system for the "majority" of merchandising firms in practice.

Professor Ijiri [5, p. 98] admits that his axiomatic system does not apply for "cost-or-market-whichever-lower method applied to inventory and marketable securities." But a limited amount of evidence available indicates that this approach is overwhelmingly the most common approach in practice. For example, in a sample of major companies the lower-of-cost-or-market method was the reported basis in 546 out of 673 instances in 1967 annual reports, and a substantial number of the other instances were combinations of both historical cost and market value pricing bases.[11]

Next let me turn to the concept of an axiom, whose general meaning is a statement or proposition which is accepted as true. (This is consistent with the definition quoted from Katz on p. 11.) In determining whether the axiom applies or is "true" in the context of accounting practice, it is necessary to interpret this asset in the particular situation. Consider the axiom on quantities. (p. 13). Implicit in this axiom is the necessity of being indifferent between identical quantities of different items in a class, i.e., elements in a class are fungible. Suppose the basic class is composed of all cash, receivables, and equities. Ijiri [5, p. 92] states:

> If cash is selected for the basic class, the value of any set of cash, regardless of whether it is cash on hand (current cash) or cash to be received or paid in future (future cash), is given by the quantity defined for the class, dollars.

At another point he [5, p. 98] states:

> An exchange involving proprietary investment must be regarded as an exchange between current cash and future cash to be delivered at an indefinite time in order to operate the system developed here and to generate a measure that approximates the one generated by the conventional accounting system, even though proprietary investment is different from loans and other payables from the standpoint of legal claims against the entity.

The treatment of cash, receivables, and equities as a single fungible class, even as an approximation of existing accounting practice, seems to be somewhat unrealistic. Current accounting standards are such that these items are not fungible items for reporting purposes. Also, exchanges in which increments and decrements affect only the basic class raises some questions. For instance, suppose a receivable is to be written off as a bad debt. The decrement of this exchange is to the basic class (reduction in receivables) offset

---

[11]American Institute of Certified Public Accountants [1].

by an equal increment in the basic class (for the reduced claim of owners on future cash). But the Value Comparison Rule does not result in a loss being recognized. Similarly a favorable cash settlement of a recorded liability would not be recognized as a gain since both the increment and decrement of the exchange affect only the basic class. On the other hand, the exchange of land or other investment not in the basic class results in a gain or loss being recognized by the Value Comparison Rule. The treatment of these items seems inconsistent.

The axiom of exchanges also raises some questions. The system applies only to situations where assets in one resource class are exchanged for assets in another resource class, presumably either because of internal modification of the resource or because of an external exchange of the resource for some other resource being brought into the firm. But it is not clear if the proposed axiom is restricted to the accepted concept of exchange. Consider the following statement:

> But in the more typical situation the degree of continuity of activity obtaining tends to prevent the finding of a basis of affinity which will permit convincing assignments, of all classes of cost incurred, to particular operations, departments, and-finally-items of product. Not all costs attach in a discernible manner, and this fact forces the accountant to fall back upon a time-period as the unit for associating certain expenses with certain revenues. Time periods are a convenience, a substitute, but the fundamental concept is unchanged. The ideal is to match costs incurred with the effects attributable to or significantly related to such costs.[12]

Thus, in assessing the relation between Professor Ijiri's axiomatic system and accounting practices, I find it difficult to assess whether or not his axiomatic structure applies mainly to some idealized version of historical costing rather than actual practices.

COMMENTS ON SANCTIONS AND LEGAL REASONING

Some of the comments made by Professor Ijiri regarding sanctions and legal reasoning were confusing to me, although time does not permit me to dwell upon each area of confusion in detail. To illustrate my point, however, consider the following quotation, "The logical analyses in accounting theories do not presuppose that accounting practices are logical." (p. 25). This is inconsistent with Professor Ijiri's earlier statements such as:

---

[12]Paton and Littleton [9, p. 15].

> The corresponding theory-building process in accounting will
> then be seen as a process of abstracting from a mass of observations
> in accounting practices... (p. 5).

Doesn't such a theory-building process "presuppose" that there is an
underlying logic in the accounting practices from which the observations
are drawn? Otherwise it would be impossible to develop a simple framework to explain the "majority" of such practices.

In this same section Professor Ijiri comments on the advantages
of an axiomatic system. I might point out in this regard that
"reasoning by example" and the judging of each transaction on "its
own merit" remain essential in applying the axiomatic system which
he has developed. For instance, the axiomatic system does not help
us in deciding which resources are under the control of an entity
or which of these resources under control are recognized as assets
by the accounting system. Nor does the axiomatic system distinguish
between what does and what does not constitute an exchange. We must
of necessity "reason by example" in interpreting what constitutes
exchanges, just as Professor Ijiri reasoned from example journal entries
in developing the Axiom of Exchanges.

It seems to me that the axiomatic system developed by Professor
Ijiri does little to resolve the major policy making problems that
currently face the accounting profession. Such problems are assumed
away in the axioms. For example, problems regarding inventory cost
allocations (FIFO versus LIFO) are assumed away by the assumption
that classes (or subclasses) exist and exchanges are identified within
these classes. The real problem, however, lies in identifying the
appropriate inventory classes and exchanges. Similarly, the axiomatic
system does very little to resolve the controversial problem of tax
allocation. The recognition of tax and other liabilities arises in
exchanges which Professor Ijiri takes as given. Whether or not the
government has a future claim on cash is left to subjective interpretation. In his system, it probably does not matter much in any
case since the system assumes indifference between owner claims and
claims of the government and creditors on assets.

CONCLUSION

May I close with another quotation from Katz [7, p. 93] which is
not given in Professor Ijiri's paper. It reads as follows:

> Moreover, it is certainly an open question how successful
> ordinary language philosophy can be in its attempt to deal with
> traditional philosophical questions if it does not cultivate the study

of language in general. . . . Hence, without a theory of language, the linguistic treatment of philosophical issues, theses, positions, and concepts is so highly restricted that even the best of analyses cannot claim to apply beyond the boundaries of the conceptual systems underlying a narrow class of languages, more often than not a class that contains just one's own native language.

It appears that Professor Ijiri has restricted his analysis to "a narrow class" of accounting journal entries. His approach and comments are most interesting but the base of his study needs to be broadened.

BIBLIOGRAPHY

[1] American Institute of Certified Public Accountants. *1968 Accounting Trends and Techniques.* New York: American Institute of Certified Public Accountants, 1968.

[2] Chambers, R. J. *Accounting, Evaluation and Economic Behavior.* Englewood Cliffs, N. J.: Prentice-Hall, Inc., 1966.

[3] Churchman, C. W. *Prediction and Optimal Decision.* Englewood Cliffs, N. J.: Prentice-Hall, Inc., 1961.

[4] Edwards, E. O., and P. W. Bell. *The Theory and Measurement of Business Income.* Berkeley, Calif.: University of California Press, 1961.

[5] Ijiri, Y. *The Foundations of Accounting Measurement: A Mathematical, Economic, and Behavioral Inquiry.* Englewood Cliffs, N.J.: Prentice-Hall Inc., 1967.

[6] Ijiri, Y. "Logic and Sanctions in Accounting." Paper presented at Accounting Colloquium I. The University of Kansas, Lawrence, Kansas. April 24–26, 1969.

[7] Katz, J. J. *Philosophy of Language.* New York: Harper and Row, 1966.

[8] Miller, D. W., and M. K. Starr. *The Structure of Human Decisions.* Englewood Cliffs, N. J.: Prentice-Hall, Inc., 1967.

[9] Paton, W. A., and A. C. Littleton. *An Introduction to Corporate Accounting Standards.* Chicago: American Accounting Association, 1940.

[10] Sprouse, R. T., and M. Moonitz. *A Tentative Set of Broad Accounting Principles for Business Enterprises.* New York: American Institute of Certified Public Accountants, 1962.

[11] Von Neumann, J., and O. Morgenstern. *Theory of Games and Economic Behavior.* Princeton: Princeton University Press, 1944.

[12] Winborne, M. G. *The Application of Sets and Symbolic Logic to Selected Accounting Principles and Practices.* Unpublished Ph.D. dissertation, University of Texas, Austin, Texas, 1962.

THE SYSTEMS APPROACH TO MEASUREMENT IN BUSINESS FIRMS

C. West Churchman

My remarks are based on a philosophical point of view, and in philosophical style, I will concentrate on the question I'd like to raise rather than any answer one might give to it.

Like all operations researchers, I have had to rely very strongly on accounting systems. I have expressed myself over the years in print and other places with considerable dissatisfaction regarding accounting systems from the point of view of the operations research practitioner. Dissatisfaction is not borne out of irritation, but rather has a real philosophical base. It is this base which I would again like to develop here. The question that I'm raising is whether the dissatisfaction is a sound one, and, if so, whether there is any hope of trying to relieve the difficulties.

The problem is that, although we probably have done reasonably well with mathematical model building in operations research, we are hopelessly bad as a science and profession as far as data collection is concerned. We simply do not have sound methods of gathering information about a firm from the point of view of trying to develop improved decision making. As a consequence, we have had to use all sorts of *ad hoc* techniques in gathering our information. This point of view is well documented by a glance at bulletins describing operations research curricula. There are no operations research courses dealing with measurement or data collection, although it is quite clear to any student that a significant part of his activities will have to be engaged in data collection. And that forecast on his part turns out to be absolutely true. Some have estimated that about 95% of an operations researcher's time is spent in trying to get information about the firm. Why is there this great difficulty in gathering information, and is there anything we can do about it?

If for a moment we make the assumption that physical science is the best prototype of measurement that man has so far developed,[1]

---

[1] I am referring, of course, to the theory of the process of measurement, and not to actual practice which often leaves much to be desired.

then we find that the social sciences, and in particular operations research, are far behind so far as this prototype is concerned. Our main weakness lies in what the physicists would call instrumentation and calibration. These two activities are essentially designed to make sure that different individuals conducting measurements in different situations will essentially come up with the same result. If the temperature or pressure changes, the calibration techniques allow the physical scientist to adjust his readings so as to attain agreement with someone who measures under different temperature or pressure conditions.

To be more specific, we need to give a statement of what measurement is like in the physical sciences. In this regard, I have drawn heavily on my philosophical mentor, Edgar Arthur Singer, who in a book entitled *Experience and Reflection*[2] lays out one of the deepest and most satisfactory accounts of how the physical sciences proceed in the process of measurement. In this paper, I do not wish to go into Singer's analysis in great depth. Essentially, Singer views measurement as a set of activities of a group of measurers who use calibration and instrumentation as communication devices. If their results are sufficiently in agreement, they conclude, all other things being equal, that the calibration and instrumentation are satisfactory. If their results do not agree within certain limits, then appropriate steps must be taken to vary the basic theories which themselves lead to variations in the calibration and instrumentation procedures.

According to Singer, there are two things that can happen if there is a group of independent observers looking at objects under different circumstances. One is that their readings, as adjusted by their theory, will all be exactly the same; that is to say, their readings are in complete agreement. And the other is that the readings will be different. Singer argues that in the physical sciences if the readings are all exactly the same, then the group of readers is instructed to take the readings out to another decimal place; that is, there is an explicit attempt on the part of the group of observers to develop readings which vary in the last decimal place. We can already see a difference between measurement in the physical sciences and measurement in the social sciences. If, for example, we look at the accounting community, it's clear that a great majority of their activities are designed to make sure that independent observers come up with exactly the same numbers.

Proceeding now with the process of measurement in the physical sciences, if the readings differ then the group attempts to find out whether the independent observers are consistent with one another.

2E. A. Singer, Jr. [2].

Tests of consistency would normally follow standard statistical procedures: one determines whether readings obtained in different places and conditions, when adjusted, are significantly different according to statistical criteria.

None of this process would be at all possible, according to Singer, unless the group of observers in the physical sciences had already committed themselves to a theory of nature, which, in our language, includes a forecast. One cannot possibly calibrate an instrument unless he does some forecasting, because the process of calibrating an instrument amounts to saying that if one were able to take an object and compare it to a standard under standard conditions, such and such things would happen. Thus in the physical sciences one does not take a body of data and make an inductive leap into the future from it. Rather, the very data that one collects has already made some commitment as to what the future, as well as the past, must be like.

It is important to emphasize that calibration is not merely a technical task to be assigned to a laboratory assistant or acting clerk. It requires the highest degree of scientific knowledge to be able to set up a calibration system.

Of course, one recognizes immediately that the process of measurement in the physical sciences is circular; one makes some assumptions about the natural world in order to take readings, i.e., to develop a calibration and instrumentation. Using these readings, one then tries to determine whether the preliminary assumptions about the nature of the natural world are true.

In the language of systems science, data collection and theory construction in the physical sciences are not separable activities. One cannot design a system to collect data without employing a fairly elaborate theory, and one cannot develop a theory without employing some kind of data.

In contrast, one finds in social science a strong assumption that these two components are, in fact, quite separable. For example, there are a number of recent books on forecasting techniques. What is striking about these texts is their implicit assumption that the social scientist *first* collects a set of data and *then* attempts (using regression and other techniques) to develop a forecast. In effect, the social scientist seems to say, "I take a set of data, I develop a regression equation, and this provides some kind of extrapolating technique." Such a philosophy of measurement is quite contrary to the basic methods of the physical scientist.

In view of the strong difference between the philosophies of measurement of the physical sciences and the social sciences, one is led naturally to ask whether the theory of measurement in the physical sciences is applicable to the social sciences. Have we, in effect, misguided ourselves by making such a strong separation between the data collection component and the theory construction component?   My assumption in this paper is that the theory of measurement in the physical sciences is the correct and ideal prototype.   As a consequence, we ought to begin to recognize that, whether we like it or not, our assumptions do get into the data that we collect.   What is necessary is that we begin to spell out what these assumptions are.

Let me illustrate the point I'm trying to make in terms of the forecast of sales.   In operations research we frequently conduct studies on inventory control; in these studies it is necessary to try to determine what the demand will be on the inventory.   The somewhat innocent operations researcher who follows the model of measurement in the social sciences described above will assume that his task is a well defined one.   Typically, he asks whether or not the company has collected information, e.g., in invoices, which can tell him by week or month the pattern of sales, say, over the past two years.   With this in hand, he will attempt to determine whether there are seasonal trends, and, if so, to try to extrapolate demand over the next two years, possibly using additional evidence indicating a growth or decay in the total amount of sales.

But a little reflection shows that this operations researcher has, in fact, made a very strong assumption about the future characteristics of the sales of the company.   He has assumed, for example, that the marketing and pricing system will operate in very much the same way as they have in the past, or, more strongly, he has assumed that the marketing and pricing system *ought* to operate as they have in the past.   If there are to be some significant changes in the marketing system, then surely a simple regression analysis on past sales is apt to be seriously wrong in view of the changes that are about to occur.

From the physical science point of view, the problem is to define what "sale" means.   Physical scientists have noted that certain measurements exhibit a great deal of stability with respect to time and place and other characteristics of the environment, while other measurements seem to vary quite drastically.   The same point of view applies to the concept of sale, which is probably a very stable concept for certain commodities and is somewhat independent of pricing, advertising, fads, and other variables, whereas sale in other cases obviously is highly dependent on the characteristics of the environment.   Consequently, one cannot determine whether an item has been "sold" until the relationship of the activity of purchasing is related to the other variables of the environment.

Of course, one could argue that "a sale is a sale," indicating thereby that whatever number is shown on an invoice is by definition the amount of the sale. Thus one might agree that operations researchers are obliged to make assumptions in order to use past records to assess future plans, but a social scientist interested only in "describing" the past need make no assumptions. To be sure, I am not interested in so-called descriptive science in this paper, but it should be pointed out that description of the past also involves the scientist in strong assumptions. For one thing, all science must be capable of handling the problem of discrepancy of observations. Thus, if one record says that a sale has been made and another says that it has not, then the scientist must have an *a priori* theory which explains the difference.

Thus, the important thing about measurement is not quantification. The essence of measurement is the very refined relationship between theory and observation.

To state the point of view in another way, in the physical science model, the physicist must necessarily bring in a presupposition about a causal linkage between events which he observes. Without such a causal linkage, he could not possibly do a proper job of calibration and instrumentation.

Many social scientists, on the other hand, show a great reluctance to make any kind of explicit causal assumption about the world until evidence for causality has been developed through the data. But the argument given above shows that in fact they do make causal assumptions implicitly.

Once we recognize that the process of data collection requires an *a priori* causal theory, then the debate about inferring causal links by means of statistical regression theory becomes futile. Here is an amusing story relative to the fallacy of equating causality with correlation. An operations research group had recommended that the advertising budget of a firm be severely cut, because they believed they had found some rather ingenious ways of using reduced advertising in strategic regions and times. The operations research group was to make a presentation to management within a few weeks. At this point, the advertising agency heard of the recommendation and asked its statistician to examine its validity. He looked over the data and decided the thing to do was to make a correlation between one period's advertising budget and the following period's sales. As a result of this analysis, he arrived at a correlation coefficient of .94. As a consequence, he felt he had the evidence he needed to show that advertising causes sales to go up, and hence that the advertising budget should not be cut.

Meanwhile, the operations research team heard about what he had been doing, and one of the group had a very clever idea. He took the two variables, one period's sales, and the next period's advertising, and conducted a correlation analysis; the result was a correlation coefficient of .99. Thus, one is led to conclude that one period's sales "causes" the next period's advertising!

Operations researchers should always make their causal models explicit. For example, a linear programming model is a causal model which assumes that if one changes an activity in a certain way, this change will cause a change in net sales or net profit. The objective function of a linear program, therefore, is not a regression equation over a set of variables collected in the past. It is based on the very strong assumption that certain changes in the characteristics of a system will cause other changes in other characteristics of the system.

To give these remarks their proper historical setting, they are very strongly based on Immanuel Kant's *Critique of Pure Reason* [1], in which Kant argued that all human observers must make causal assumptions about the nature of the world in which they live, or else experience itself would be meaningless. Kant's philosophical thesis is seen to be quite valid in connection with all of the activities of the operations researchers or social scientists who are trying to understand enough about organization to be able to make recommendations for their improvement. Of course, one has to rewrite Kant's *Critique of Pure Reason* to do the job as we see it today, because Kant believed that his *a priori* assumptions were necessary and therefore fixed, while we recognize them to be strategic assumptions that are chosen by the measurer and subject to change in terms of subsequent events.

In conclusion, another way to state my thesis is to say that current accounting practice is essentially independent of the practice of theorizing about organizations. The accountants, to be sure, use a modicum of theory, as in developing cost accounting techniques, but the assumptions that are at least explicitly made within cost accounting about the nature of the system are extremely narrow ones. As a consequence, the operations researcher has no really valid reason for assuming that the data being collected by the cost accounting system is the kind of data that is appropriate in the development of the measurements which he requires in order to arrive at optimal recommendations.

I realize that the practicing accountant will point out that his data is used for reasons other than supporting operations research activities. He is probably right with respect to the legal requirements of the firm. But there is one defense of his practice which I do not think can be taken as falling outside the scope of my remarks in this paper. The accountant often says that he is trying to generate information which will be "useful" to the manager in his decision making. But this is exactly what the operations researcher is trying to do. If my thesis is correct that the operations researcher cannot develop better data without making strong assumptions about the characteristics of the system, then surely this must be also true of the manager and of the accounting system which is trying to develop "useful data." And if accounting data is of questionable value to the operations researcher, then it is also of questionable value to the manager's decision making function.

My remarks in this paper have been intentionally provocative. The purpose of the provocation is to raise the question of whether it is possible to convert some sections of accounting practice into something that begins to approximate a measurement system.

To avoid confusion, I should point out that calibration is not simply a laboratory technician's job. It is an extremely elaborate and difficult task, requiring a great deal of expert knowledge of the discipline. As one reads the history of a concept like "length," for example, one finds that the very best minds in the world were required to develop the proper calibration techniques.

To be sure, accounting is a systematic method of gathering data. And of course, this is much to its credit. But to be systematic in gathering data does not mean to measure, under the assumptions that I have made.

What I've been trying to say can be expressed as a hope. I hope our science can develop a theory of the firm which would be the basis for deciding upon the appropriate instruments, calibration techniques, and observational procedures to be used in measuring the critical aspects of the firm. The result would then be a set of "data" which would indicate whether or not the theory we started is correct. If not, I hope we will develop the criteria to tell us how the theory should be changed. The changed theory would then generate new instruments, new calibration methods, and new data. Then we could say that we have a system which measures.

BIBLIOGRAPHY

[1] Kant, Immanuel. *Critique of Pure Reason.* 1781.
[2] Singer, E. A., Jr. *Experience and Reflection.* Edited by C. West Churchman. Philadelphia: University of Pennsylvania Press, 1959.

THE SYSTEMS APPROACH TO MEASUREMENT IN BUSINESS FIRMS

CRITIQUE

William W. Cooper

Dr. George Kozmetsky — a CPA who is now Dean of the School of Business at the University of Texas — once told me that he made it a rule never to follow West Churchman on any program. The foolhardiness of not following this advice should be apparent, and it is even worse to be put in the position of a discussant of a paper such as he has just presented.

In addition to these strategic difficulties there are also some tactical ones which I have encountered. Dr. Churchman's paper was not completed in time for this conference and so I had to prepare my remarks from the summary abstract he sent me. His talk deviated from the abstract and it also differed (to a lesser extent) from the final version of his paper. Since his presentation stimulated a lively and interesting discussion at this conference, it would seem that some effort should be made to preserve aspects of this discussion and I, therefore, am adapting my own conference remarks with these considerations in mind.

Professor Yuji Ijiri was one of the participants in this very lively discussion and, hence, it seems apt to quote from his recently published book, *The Foundations of Accounting Measurement*, in order to establish the timeliness as well as the relevance and significance of Dr. Churchman's remarks for their bearing on present states of knowledge and practice in accounting.

> Within the complex of the modern business community, accounting has come to face the challenges of such disciplines as computer technology, operations research techniques, behavioral science theories, etc. In relating its unique manner of approach to the services and organization it performs for business, it is essential that accountants have a clear idea of its own discipline, its own long-developed and refined philosophy. . . .

> . . . Accounting has now come to a critical turning point which is at least as important as the one it came to in the early 1930's. Accountants must respond to the challenges. But the response

should come after a careful study of the foundations upon which accounting has been constructed. . . .[1]

This all suggests that it is prudent to consider where we are as well as where we ought to want to go in light of Dr. Churchman's suggestions. Thus, in particular, we need to know how far we have gone in our development of "a theory of a firm" or at least in our procedures (or paradigms) for validating such a theory and its related measurements in any applicable case.

In areas like systems design we have gone somewhat further, I think, than Dr. Churchman indicates, but not as far as we should — or can, without altering our procedures. In fact, some years ago David Rosenblatt and I joined with Eric Kohler in an attempt to define such terms as "theories," "axioms," and "measurement" for inclusion in the latter's *A Dictionary for Accountants*,[2] where we observed that, *inter alia,* choices between theories needed to depend on their tendency to lead to the discovery of new problems or facts — but then we noted that "new theories or new problem areas of accounting have seldom emerged from theories of system design."

I believe that it is the latter property that Dr. Churchman refers to when he says that accountants "use a modicum of theory, as in developing cost accounting techniques, but the assumptions that are at least explicitly made within cost accounting about the nature of the system are extremely narrow ones. . . ." It is in the area of system theorizing and design, however, that the main challenges are being encountered, and hence it is this area that is most in need of attention.

Some things may be done immediately in extending present accounting methods and approaches to accommodate these challenges. For instance, A. Charnes and I [1] suggested extending the record-keeping concepts of accounting to comprehend the models (if any) employed by OR analysts or others in the service of a business firm. This means that the models and their subsequent uses, non-uses, or misuses, as well as the appropriateness of their constructions, would be subject to audit as part of the usual control and evaluation procedures in accounting. Presumably this would embrace the "opportunity cost" dimensions of such models, including the alternatives, considered or not, in the processes of model synthesis.

I should perhaps underscore the fact that these OR models have, to date at least, been mainly restricted to the *planning* dimensions of management. Many of them have also been oriented toward a hypothetical individual decision maker and to decision processes reminiscent of those used in the model of the firm in classical economics.

---

[1]The quotation is from the dust jacket of *The Foundations of Accounting Measurement* [3].
[2]Kohler [5, p. 493].

This is not adequate to the kinds of systems models required for an accounting, however, in which a multiplicity of decision makers operate to influence each other's behavior, as well as the data, the parameters and other aspects of the environments that each is required to consider.   Parenthetically, one might note that this kind of "individual decision-maker" model is also implicit in the kinds of independence assumed for the testing and verification procedures used in physics — whereas in accounting many aspects of the audit and verification procedures influence the behavior of pertinent officials as well as the data they encounter. Indeed, the latter types of considerations — viz., the influence of one person's behavior on another's premises and data — underlie some relatively recent research such as the studies of N. C. Churchill [2] and A. Stedry [6] in, respectively, "behavioral audits" and "motivational costs." These studies, in turn, suggest something even more than is implied by Dr. Churchman's admission that accounting must supply multiple types of data for different purposes as well as for the multiple objectives that it may be called upon to service.[3] They suggest possibilities which include incorporating such personal properties and propensities as part of an accounting system.

I wonder whether Dr. Churchman would agree that if these suggested developments were joined to his, they would together point toward an "automatic management" concept in which all decisions would be implied by the design of the accounting (data) system. To be sure, some of this is true even now. However, the indicated further development would raise this to an explicit level in which decision consequences would all be considered and evaluated as data system designs were prescribed ar.d altered. Questions of uncertainty and assumptions of responsibility would need to be resolved, of course, but in a real sense the problems of management would then emerge as problems in data system design, along with related controls and evaluation procedures.   This, too, would then become part of the theory construction tasks to which Dr. Churchman is inviting attention by accounting researchers, who would then need to extend relevant parts of the behavioral sciences as well as the practices and theories in mathematical modeling.

---

[3]Erik Johnsen [4].

BIBLIOGRAPHY

[1] Charnes, A., and W. W. Cooper. "Some Network Characterizations for Mathematical Programming and Accounting Approaches to Planning and Control." *Accounting Review,* Vol. XLII, No. 1 (January, 1967), pp. 24–52. Reprinted in John L. Livingstone (editor) *Management Planning and Control: Mathematical Models.* New York: McGraw-Hill, Inc., 1970.

[2] Churchill, Neil C. "Behavioral Effects of an Audit: An Experimental Study." Unpublished Ph.D. dissertation, University of Michigan, Ann Arbor, 1962.

[3] Ijiri, Yuji. *The Foundations of Accounting Measurement.* Englewood Cliffs, N.J.: Prentice-Hall, Inc., 1967.

[4] Johnsen, Erik. *Studies in Multi-objective Decision Models,* Monograph No. 1. Economic Research Center, University of Lund, Sweden, 1968.

[5] Kohler, Eric. *A Dictionary for Accountants.* 3d ed. Englewood Cliffs, N.J.: Prentice-Hall, Inc., 1963.

[6] Stedry, A. *Budget Control and Cost Behavior.* Englewood Cliffs, N.J.: Prentice-Hall, Inc., 1960.

THE SYSTEMS APPROACH TO MEASUREMENT IN BUSINESS FIRMS

CRITIQUE

Kermit D. Larson

Professor Churchman has identified four necessary components of a measurement system: (1) instruments (including their calibration); (2) qualified users of the instruments who make observations; (3) qualified examiners of the observations who estimate their internal reliability; and (4) qualified theoreticians who estimate when, where, and how the measurements ought to be used. Regarding the fourth component, that is, qualified theoreticians who estimate when, where, and how the measurements ought to be used, I assume we would accept a set of statements which adequately prescribe the when, where, and how, even though the qualified theoretician also happened to be the qualified user or examiner. At any rate, the point is well taken that a measurement system is incomplete if it does not include some means of relating the procedures of measuring to a descriptive or explanatory model that can be of use to decision makers. It seems to me that the function of this component — of recognizing underlying theoretical assumptions — is to relate the procedures of measurement to the decision making process.

THE COMPONENTS OF ACCOUNTING MEASUREMENT SYSTEMS: A LACK OF INTEGRATION

One subject which may be worthy of further comment is the idea that the components of an accounting measurement system are not adequately integrated. In particular, the component which estimates when, where, and how the measurements ought to be used is viewed as being somehow separated from the other components of the measurement system. To suggest this separation of components is an interesting and, I would suggest, fruitful way of describing and attacking the problem of accounting measures having limited and/or questionable significance to decision makers. It was at one time popular to argue that accountants had no business worrying about the descriptive significance of their reports to decision makers. The question of how accounting information should be used was frequently viewed as the responsibility of the user. So long as the accountant would fully disclose the procedures he employed, his responsibility was satisfied in this regard.

It would not appear to be a very enlightened view of accounting to argue that this general position is as prevalent now as it apparently was some years ago. If there have been any noticeable changes in accounting thought in recent years, one which must stand out is the shift in attention away from the rather positivistic approach of attempting to isolate and report the "facts" of business activity (whatever that means) toward the more normative effort of developing measurement and reporting techniques that can somehow be rationalized as being relevant to decision makers. We are now at least giving lip service to a so-called "user orientation." And there have been, and continue to be, serious attempts to develop the theoretical links between a specification of measurement procedures and decision making processes. But it seems safe to say that this change in direction has not yet provided any landmark breakthroughs, either in terms of developing new measurements that are unusually valuable to decision makers or in terms of developing new rationalizations of existing measurements which radically improve our notions of when, where, and how the measurements ought to be used.

It goes without saying that our change in orientation — our recognition that measurement is a purposive activity — has not been complete. In many respects, the system component which decides the "when, where, and how" issue is separated from the other components. Financial analysis, for example, is generally approached as something which assumes and follows the specification of measurement procedures. Further, this function is often fulfilled by people who do not participate directly in the development of the measurements. Thus, it continues to be a problem that the first three components of the measurement system are designed without adequate consideration being given to the "when, where, and how" component. Accounting seems to have progressed in this regard, but it has been a very slow evolutionary process.

It might be argued that the measurement components: (1) of instrumentation (and I interpret that as including the specification of procedures); (2) of qualified users of the instruments; and (3) of qualified examiners, substantially circumscribe the accounting function, as that function is historically and often currently perceived. The prescriptions of when, where, and how have fallen largely within the domains of other disciplines, such as finance, operations research, and to a certain extent the behavioral sciences. To the extent that this is true, accounting has wandered about without much direction.

At the same time, some of these other areas appear to bring forth a variety of decision models and analyses which lack the essential measurement system components that comprise accounting.

This line of reasoning leads to a conclusion that is almost trite in the context of this colloquium. It suggests that if the development of a so-called "complete" measurement system is to occur, within which the components are adequately integrated, it lies substantially beyond what we typically ascribe as the bounds of accounting. It requires an integration of disciplines, and more particularly an integration at the stage of system construction. And this cannot be accomplished, I would not think, by attempting to integrate what we might call the "results" of these areas of separate investigation. In a sense, I suppose, if these disciplines are integrated before their individual results are obtained, then each of the disciplines loses its separate identification with respect to that particular investigation. Conceivably, we could then talk in terms of a more complete information system and possibly even a discipline which describes that area.

THEORETICAL ASSUMPTIONS IN TRADITIONAL ACCOUNTING SYSTEMS

Before we conclude that the traditional efforts of the accountants are totally unfounded on theoretical assumptions, we may wish to reconsider the problem of separation between the components of an accounting measurement system. Separation of components is a relative problem — it is not absolute. The traditional accounting procedures relating generally to historical cost, and the several deviations therefrom, *have* been based on numerous theoretical assumptions concerning the informational needs of decision makers. They have often been handed down, I admit, in very authoritative statements which now appear at times quite dubious. They frequently espouse concepts that are believed to be significant with respect to the decision making process, but tend to accept those concepts as rather primitive terms and not really analyze how they work — how they relate to the decision making process or how the accounting procedure relates to the concepts.[1] Nevertheless, these statements do involve assumptions which provide some basis for the development of measurement procedures. And it could be argued that they have gained varying degrees of validity through continued use and modification in more or less successful firms. It seems that our primary shortcoming has

---

[1]An example is Littleton's notion that historical cost represents investment [2, pp. 23-4]. The concept of "investment" presumably has significance to the decision maker. However, if one analyzes what is meant by investment, one is led directly back to price aggregates, and this doesn't seem to take us very far in terms of explicating our assumptions.

been not so much a lack of assumptions as a failure to work out their significance, thereby making the assumptions explicit, and a general inability to provide some sort of empirical verification of our implied predictions of user behavior.

THE LACK OF VARIATION IN ACCOUNTING MEASUREMENTS

Another problem that deserves further consideration is the point that accounting methods result in a single number. Because our methods do not provide divergent measurements of a property, we are essentially incapable of assessing the accuracy of our measurements in any precise manner.

In one sense, it is certainly true that accounting methods do not provide variation in measurements; in another sense, it is not true. Different accountants come up with widely varying numbers. The problem seems to be that we are limited to only one observation. The potential variation in accounting measurements stems from different usages of instrumentation. Accounting is not designed to allow repeated observations with repeated applications of the same instrumentation. We have not yet defined (and I agree that it is a problem of definition) concepts in a manner which allow repeated observations using the same instrumentation.

There is possibly another way of looking at this problem. If accounting is viewed as an information processing system with business activity serving as the source of data and decision processes serving as the destination of accounting information, the problem is as follows: within the accounting process there are a number of points at which an important relationship between concepts can only be *presumed*. In order to move from a set of measurement procedures to a concept that is identified with the decision making process, one is forced to make a presumptive leap of faith. For example, Chambers' definition of financial position can be identified with a model of decision making. He defines financial position as "the capacity of an entity at a point of time for engaging in exchanges."[2] By comparison, the statement of financial position can only be defined in terms of the procedures that were utilized to arrive at the statement. There is a tremendous leap of faith that must occur before we can assume that one at all approximates the other.

This is not, I understand, a problem that is unique to accounting, but it is certainly one that plagues accounting. We have not yet isolated or identified more than a few of the points at which we must

---

[2]Raymond J. Chambers [1, p. 81].

make these presumptive leaps of faith. Careful identification of these points would not eliminate the problem that accounting methods preclude variations in numerical results. It may, however, lead to an improved definitional approach to the concepts we are attempting to measure. And the lack of variation in accounting measurements is, I believe, a reflection of inadequate definitions.

A GENERAL IMPLICATION

Professor Churchman's analysis raises a number of questions. Perhaps its most significant implication for accounting is the implication that accounting researchers may not have been asking the right questions. It is not that accounting stands without a vast array of unanswered questions; they exist in great numbers. But answers are likely to be empty if the sequence of questions is not in order; it could even ensue that they were the wrong questions.

BIBLIOGRAPHY

[1] Chambers, Raymond J. *Accounting, Evaluation and Economic Behavior*. Englewood Cliffs, N.J.: Prentice-Hall, Inc., 1966.
[2] Littleton, A. C. *Structure of Accounting Theory*. Urbana, Illinois: American Accounting Association, 1953.

PART II
Expanding Perspectives in Contemporary Accounting Research

THE BEHAVIOR OF "BEHAVIORAL" ACCOUNTANTS

Selwyn Becker

Before I get into my paper, I would like you to seriously consider a segment from a Sidney Harris column in the *Chicago Daily News*, March 25, 1969.

> Theodore Sturgeon, an excellent science fiction writer, was once asked by an interviewer why so much science fiction is bad. 'Well,' replied Sturgeon, 'ninety percent of science fiction is rubbish because ninety percent of everything is rubbish.'

I bring Sturgeon's assertion to your attention because today I will evaluate some statements I made about accounting and accountants two years ago. If after evaluating those statements I am forced to conclude that ninety percent of what I said was rubbish, don't judge me too harshly; I will have come up to the universal standard.

Two years ago I participated in the annual Conference on Empirical Research in Accounting as a discussant for Doris Cook's paper, "The Effect of Frequency of Feedback on Attitude and Performance."[1]

Despite the fact that I knew no accounting at that time, I stated that accounting was merely a collection of sometimes followed rules, but that potentially it was a discipline within the behavioral sciences. In order to realize that potential, accountants should, I continued, begin building theory and deducing testable hypotheses. Further, I stated that accounting was a coding-transmission-receiving system and that behavioral accounting theory should be concerned with regularities and irregularities in the coding and receiving processes. By that I meant business events occur and accountants aggregate and code (in an information theory sense) these events; and sometimes they do so in different ways. Some accountants use accelerated depreciation where others might use straight line; some use LIFO for inventory valuation where others advocate FIFO.

Accountants, being people, do not always describe business events the same way. That is differential coding. By the same token,

---

[1]See Doris Cook [12, pp. 213–24], and Selwyn Becker [2, pp. 225–28].

69

because receivers of the coded information are human, even if coding is held constant, people receive different amounts of information and different messages from coded, transmitted material. It was my position that the psychologist properly should be concerned with how and why people's motives are changed, while the accountant should be interested in how and why, because people have motives, the coding-transmission-receiving is modified.

Today, I want to evaluate my caveat to the accounting profession by reviewing and critically examining the accounting research relevant to it. At this point, it really is appropriate to acknowledge the help of my colleagues. Dealing with unfamiliar variables, my colleagues' aid is and was indispensable. So for the time they spent and the advice given, I want to publicly thank Bill Beaver, Nick Dopuch, and David Green.

First, I want to look at the research dealing with differences in the amount and kind of information that people, as decision makers, receive from the coded, transmitted material. The largest number of studies which can be said to have a behavioral science orientation or which make use of behavioral or social science techniques are in this category of research. Typically, the researcher coded some information in two or more ways and then determined how those coding differences affected decision making. There are seven such studies — two by William Bruns, three by Thomas Dyckman, one by Robert Jensen, and one by Abdellatif Khemakhem. Since Bruns comes first in the alphabet, he also comes first in my review. Bruns [7] asked subjects to play a business game in a laboratory setting where they made price, advertising, and production decisions. The subjects were divided into three groups: one receiving a balance sheet with a LIFO method of inventory valuation, one with FIFO, and one with direct costing. Bruns concluded that, essentially, the different methods of inventory valuation did not affect decisions. This is not too surprising a result. Bruns never presented any hypothetical reasons why inventory valuation, which affects reported earnings, should affect the kinds of decisions he asked his subjects to make, and if they should, in what way. Bruns [6] used the same game in a second study wherein he investigated the effects on decisions of receiving an annual report compared with quarterly reports. Again, he had no theory, no explicit hypothesis, and no differences. The no differences finding could be attributed to the fact that from the statistics necessary to the play of the game, subjects could gain enough information so that interim reports added nothing to the decision maker's information. In both studies, Bruns first assumed that certain accounting variables have important effects on various kinds of business decisions. He then tested whether alternative estimates of those variables affected decisions.

The lack of differences can be attributed either to the fact that the variables are not important in decision making or that differences in the variable due to the estimating techniques were not material. We do not know which is correct.

Dyckman's [15] first study was also a laboratory situation where subjects were asked to make an investment decision by specifying dollars per share for two firms, one whose inventory was valued on a FIFO basis and one on a LIFO basis. Subjects were not given information sufficient to adjust for the different methods so the differences in reported earnings produced differences in price per share.

In his second study, Dyckman [16] added operating data to the subject's store of information, and he then found that differences in inventory valuation did not affect decision making. This time, however, his subjects made operating decisions on advertising, production, R & D, price, and dividends rather than an investment decision, as had been the case with the first study. Thus, it was impossible to determine if the no differences were due to the added information or to the different decision.

Dyckman's [17] third study was designed to answer questions left unanswered by the first two studies. Subjects were asked to evaluate firms as purchase opportunities and to assign dollar values to each firm. Different methods of valuing inventory made a difference. However, when a few subjects were also given operating data, the differences seemed to disappear.

Jensen [18] addressed himself to a similar problem. He varied depreciation and inventory methods on balance sheets mailed to financial analysts who were asked to make portfolio recommendations. Jensen found all main effects significant and no relevant interaction effects. Jensen [18, p. 237] speculates that "as in most real world situations, it would have been a hopeless task for an analyst to have tried to have placed the financial reports on a common accounting basis." Presumably, then, we can conclude that when a coding technique changes a number that is relevant to a decision, and the decision maker does not have enough information to evaluate the coding mechanism, different coding techniques will lead to different decisions. This could have been determined in a single, well controlled experiment.

I made this conclusion before discussing the final piece of research in the "coding effects decisions" category because that study adds nothing to our knowledge. Khemakhem [19] devised a business game and used financial business executives from Ohio as his subjects. He instructed half of his subjects to maximize funds and half of them to maximize earnings. He then proceeded to demonstrate that subjects instructed to maximize funds use funds statements more frequently than those instructed to maximize earnings. The latter group used earnings statements more frequently. Those volunteer subjects sound like nice, cooperative people, don't they? They certainly follow directions.

Some other conclusions were also made about use of fund statements, but since all of the conclusions were based on Chi Square Tables with inflated N's, the conclusions, whatever they were, are irrelevant. I describe this research rather than ignore it, because some accountants think highly of it. It was a winning paper in the American Accounting Association's manuscript contest for 1967.

The second category of research deals with the input side of the system: differences in coding the business events. There are four studies that I know of in this category: two by T. Ross Archibald, William H. Beaver, George H. Sorter, and me; one by Archibald; and one by Fred Neumann. In the first study, on which I collaborated, we found that financial executives' scores on an authoritarianism scale could predict whether the firm used one set of books for tax and another set for accounting purposes, or whether they used one set for both purposes.[2] The second study replicated the findings of the first study, although an intolerance or ambiguity scale was substituted for the authoritarianism measure.[3] In addition, we found that the depreciation decisions correlated with the defensive position of the firm as that position was reflected by certain financial ratios.

Archibald [1] investigated changes in depreciation decisions and found some support for the hypothesis that changes were made, at least partly, to smooth income. I interpret that to mean that managerial motives influence coding decisions as much as does the desire to transmit information.

Neumann investigated auditors' behavior and he found great inconsistencies in their noting of exceptions.[4] Auditors in different offices of the same public accounting firm followed different policies; policies differed within and between industries. In fact, whether a change was deemed material or not seemed to be entirely up to the discretion of the individual auditor.

A final category of research deals not with financial accounting, but with managerial accounting. To my knowledge, there are five studies in this category: one each by Doris M. Cook, Andrew C. Stedry, Edwin H. Caplan, Neil C. Churchill and William W.

---

[2]George H. Sorter, Selwyn W. Becker, T. Ross Archibald, and William H. Beaver [23, pp. 183–96].

[3]George H. Sorter, Selwyn W. Becker, T. Ross Archibald, and William H. Beaver [22, pp. 200–210].

[4]Neumann [20, pp. 1–17]. See also [21].

Cooper, and Don T. De Coster and John P. Fertakis. Since I already have commented extensively on Cook's and Stedry's papers elsewhere, I will not repeat myself here.[5]

Caplan [8] set out to compare managerial philosophies of 20 management accountants with those of 20 non-accounting managers, and he found no differences. He also wanted to determine the degree to which those philosophies reflected traditional or modern organization theory assumptions about behavior. He never adequately described his sample, but that is only a minor criticism of his exposition. More serious was his lack of preparation in specifying hypotheses as to why accounting managers should differ from non-accounting managers. Were the expected differences due to differences in background, in training, in personality? Were differences to be expected at the level of verbal expressions of general managerial philosophies? By that I mean, would they verbalize different norms and attitudes about management, or would they express similar norms, but because of differences in training and points of view, operationalize those norms differently? Without first thinking about these issues, Caplan developed a questionnaire which almost precluded finding any differences. Except for a few questions, the very general nature of his questions almost demands a socially desirable response. By a socially desirable response, I mean something like the following: if one were to survey all managers and ask them to predict the responses which most other managers or stockholders would consider right or proper, then we would have what we could call a social desirability scale for managerial philosophy. The responses to Caplan's questionnaire look exactly like a social desirability scale. One of the relevant observations one can make from Caplan's data is that accountants and non-accountants see the role of management accounting, or think they should see it, both as a control and motivating device.

Churchill and Cooper [9] addressed themselves to a related portion of this problem; i.e., the perceptions people have of the internal audit, the auditors, and the audit's perceived effect on behavior. Churchill and Cooper [9, p. 774] say, "almost 75 percent of the respondents indicated either a neutral or a positive attitude toward the internal auditor and the internal audit." Their statement is fairly accurate. It is also accurate to state, based on their own data, that 63 percent of the respondents are neutral or negative toward the audit, and 74 percent are neutral or negative toward auditors. Using their own data, I can come to an opposite conclusion. Such a contradiction is not too

---

[5]Doris Cook's paper can be found in [12, pp. 213–24]. Stedry's papers include [24] and [25]. Discussion of Stedry's work can be found in Selwyn W. Becker and David Green, Jr. [3] and [4].

serious if you realize that most of their conclusions are based on only a 60 percent response rate from their initially small sample of 66 people. In other words, about 40 percent of the people refused to answer the questions when they felt threatened. The answers they gave, I presume, either are socially desirable or relatively harmless. The more meaningful ones were withheld. With such poor interviewing techniques, no conclusions are possible.

Finally, DeCoster and Fertakis [13] studied budget induced pressure and supervisory behavior. They cite some studies in which it is concluded that considerate supervisory behavior is associated with efficiency. They assume, without documentation or reasoning, that budget induced pressure on the supervisor induces him to behave in an inconsiderate fashion toward his subordinates. They found that budget induced pressure was positively correlated with subordinates' ratings of considerateness of supervisors. They then performed some dubious statistical manipulations in an attempt to explain their data. They should have been better advised to discuss the derivation of their hypothesis.

Summing up to this point, we know that because of psychological or motivational reasons, people code business events differently; and because of differences in intelligence, perception, and motivation, people respond differently to the same business events when they are differentially coded and transmitted and are relevant to the decision at hand.

Let us for the moment assume that we have great confidence in these conclusions. Does that represent implementation of my caveat that behavioral accounting should begin theory building and testing in an attempt to explain interactions between coders, the accountants, and receivers, or decision makers, and the business events being transmitted? If not, then how can the caveat be implemented? It is obvious that the collection of differences just discussed do not constitute a theory. Could a theory be constructed? Yes, if it is recognized that the differences arose because of differences in the mode of structures of constructors and receivers of the information. If accounting made some assumptions about commonalities in goal structure, which are already demonstrated to be too diverse to be a feasible course of action, or if accounting arbitrarily imposed goal structures they thought desirable, then a theory, both normative and descriptive could be constructed. Carl Devine [14], in his article, "Research Methodology and Accounting Theory Formation," adopted that position. He wrote:

> . . . This writer is committed to the doctrine that the first order of business in constructing a theoretical system for a service

> function is to establish the purpose and objectives of the func-
> tion. . . . Once this first step is taken, we have a framework that lets
> us investigate and conduct research in terms of carefully constructed
> objectives. . . . to argue in a vacuum that depreciation should or
> should not be recorded by a community hospital is a flagrant
> waste of intellectual efforts. Accountants . . . can make a small
> contribution by recognizing their social responsibilities, and build-
> ing their practical structure to help fulfill these responsibilities. The
> most urgent field for accounting research may not be related to
> problems concerned with the efficient measurement of transaction
> flows unless efficiency itself is defined in terms of the accomplish-
> ment of socially worthy objectives. [14, p. 399].

Well, I do not know any more about accounting now than I did
two years ago, but at least I have thought a little more about the
problem. I would ask Devine what right accountants have to specify
goals, either for society or even less broadly for the senders or
receivers of accounting data. My answer is that they have none, at
least no more than any other individual. So what of my caveat in
which I implicitly, and I now believe wrongly, adopted Devine's
position? Now I would recommend that financial accounting be concerned with building middle range descriptive theory. By that I
mean accountants should develop logical explanations for why decisions are made. For instance, under what conditions will an accounting manager decide to change methods of valuing inventory or depreciation? How do these decisions relate to other significant business
events like investment in R & D, ratios of fixed to variable costs,
diversification, and other such decisions? How will the differences
in coding affect users of accounting information? Which decisions
will be affected and under what conditions?

The proper function of such a middle range theory, in my opinion,
would be to implement Vatter's position:

> The financial statements are the reports of the management
> about the corporation. These reports are directed to all inter-
> ested parties, without preference or prejudice, and no attempt is
> made to meet the specific needs or concerns of particular groups
> in these reports.[6]

Behavioral accounting research demonstrates that decisions are
affected by different reporting techniques; it is then prejudiced not
to describe the events using all the techniques. In other words,
within this framework of impartial coding and transmission of business
events, behavioral accounting can define variances in accounting

---

[6]Vatter has expressed his views concerning financial reporting in various places, especially
[26, pp. 71–87], and [27, pp. 179–97].

as a function of motives and variable behavior as a function of accounting differences. The middle range descriptive theory defines the minimum amounts and kinds of information which must be transmitted in order to be objective and unprejudiced.

That function of middle range theory does not completely define the role of behavioral accounting because in managerial accounting, the goals are to control, change, and motivate behavior. All cost control systems, including performance standards and evaluations, budgets, variances, and transfer pricing, are areas in which accountants and organization theorists together should develop theory and test hypotheses about the interaction of accounting systems and the human response to those systems. For instance, under what conditions are the budgeted goals internalized by managers and employees? Are there differences in employee functioning when budgets define goals in terms of maximum costs or in terms of minimum sales or profits? Are a manager's inventory policies different when he is evaluated as a profit center versus as a cost center? These are just examples of some questions that could be investigated.

Finally, and a new caveat, the goals will never be reached unless the profession, the accounting profession, develops some method of evaluating behavioral accounting research. It is obvious that the journals, the editors, and even the judges for prize manuscripts are not trained in behavioral or even experimental sciences. The profession needs an alliance with some scientists willing to perform an evaluation function for the accounting profession until accountants themselves become trained in these areas.

Before I finish, I want to say that I hope this paper will not be described as Coase describes the work of Pigou:

> It is strange that a doctrine as faulty as that developed by Pigou should have been so influential, although part of its success has probably been due to lack of clarity in the exposition. Not being clear, it was never clearly wrong. Curiously enough, this obscurity in the source has not prevented the emergence of a fairly well-defined oral tradition. What economists think they learn from Pigou, and what they tell their students, which I term the Pigouvian tradition, is reasonably clear. I propose to show the inadequacy of this Pigouvian tradition by demonstrating that both the analysis and the policy conclusions which it supports are incorrect.[7]

I hope that my exposition is sufficiently lucid that a relatively rapid judgment can be made as to whether or not this paper, too, comes up to the universal standard 90 percent rubbish.

---

[7]R. H. Coase [11, p. 39].

BIBLIOGRAPHY

[1] Archibald, T. Ross. "The Return to Straight-Line Depreciation: An Analysis of a Change in Accounting Method." *Empirical Research in Accounting: Selected Studies, 1967.* Chicago: The Institute of Professional Accounting, Graduate School of Business, University of Chicago, 1968.

[2] Becker, Selwyn W. "Discussion of The Effect of Frequency of Feedback on Attitudes and Performance." *Empirical Research in Accounting: Selected Studies, 1967.* Chicago: The Institute of Professional Accounting, Graduate School of Business, University of Chicago, 1968.

[3] Becker, Selwyn W., and David Green, Jr. "Budgeting and Employee Behavior." *Journal of Business,* Vol. XXXV, No. 4 (October, 1962), pp. 392-402.

[4] ——————. "Budgeting and Employee Behavior: A Rejoinder to A 'Reply'." *Journal of Business,* Vol. XXXVII, No. 2 (April, 1964), pp. 203-205.

[5] Bruns, William J., Jr. "Accounting Information and Decision-Making: Some Behavioral Hypotheses." *Accounting Review,* Vol. XLIII, No. 3 (July, 1968), pp. 469-80.

[6] ——————. "The Accounting Period Concept and Its Effect on Management." *Empirical Research in Accounting: Selected Studies, 1966.* Chicago: The Institute of Professional Accounting, Graduate School of Business, University of Chicago, 1967.

[7] ——————. "Inventory Valuation and Management Decisions." *Accounting Review,* Vol. XL, No. 2 (April, 1965), pp. 345-357.

[8] Caplan, Edwin H. "Behavioral Assumptions of Management Accounting — Report of a Field Study." *Accounting Review,* Vol. XLIII, No. 2 (April, 1968), pp. 342-62.

[9] Churchill, Neil C., and William W. Cooper. "A Field Study of Internal Auditing." *Accounting Review,* Vol. XL, No. 4 (October, 1965), pp. 767-81.

[10] Churchill, Neil C., William W. Cooper, and Trevor Sainsbury. "Laboratory and Field Studies of the Behavioral Effects of Audits." *Management Controls: New Directions in Basic Research,* edited by Charles P. Bonini, Robert K. Jaedicke, and Harvey M. Wagner. New York: McGraw-Hill, Inc., 1964.

[11] Coase, R. H. "The Problem of Social Cost." *The Journal of Law and Economics,* Vol. III (October, 1960), pp. 1-44.

[12] Cook, Doris M. "The Effect of Frequency of Feedback on Attitudes and Performance." *Empirical Research in Accounting: Selected Studies, 1967.* Chicago: The Institute of Professional Accounting, Graduate School of Business, University of Chicago, 1968.

[13] DeCoster, Don T., and John P. Fertakis. "Budget-Induced Pressure and Its Relationship to Supervisory Behavior." *Journal of Accounting Research,* Vol. VI, No. 2 (Autumn, 1968), pp. 237-46.

[14] Devine, Carl Thomas. "Research Methodology and Accounting Theory Formulation." *Accounting Review,* Vol. XXXV, No. 2 (July, 1960), pp. 387-99.

[15] Dyckman, Thomas R. "On the Investment Decision." *Accounting Review,* Vol. XXXIX, No. 2 (April, 1964), pp. 285-95.

[16] ――――――. "The Effects of Alternative Accounting Techniques on Certain Management Decisions." *Journal of Accounting Research,* Vol. 2, No. 1 (Spring, 1964), pp. 91-107.

[17] ――――――. "On the Effects of Earnings-trend, Size, and Inventory Valuation Procedures in Evaluating a Business Firm." *Research in Accounting Measurement,* edited by Robert K. Jaedicke, Yuji Ijiri, and Oswald Nielsen. Evanston, Illinois: American Accounting Association, 1966.

[18] Jensen, Robert E. "An Experimental Design for Study of Effects of Accounting Variations in Decision Making." *Journal of Accounting Research,* Vol. IV, No. 2 (Autumn, 1966), pp. 224-38.

[19] Khemakhem, Abdellatif. "A Simulation of Management-Decision Behavior: 'Funds' and Income." *Accounting Review,* Vol. XLIII, No. 3 (July, 1968), pp. 522-34.

[20] Neumann, Frederick L. "The Auditing Standard of Consistency." *Empirical Research in Accounting: Selected Studies, 1968.* Chicago: The Institute of Professional Accounting, Graduate School of Business, University of Chicago, 1969.

[21] ――――――. "The Incidence and Nature of Consistency Exceptions." *Accounting Review,* Vol. XLIV, No. 3 (July, 1969), pp. 546-54.

[22] Sorter, George H., Selwyn W. Becker, T. Ross Archibald and William H. Beaver. "Accounting and Financial Measures as Indicators of Corporate Personality — Some Empirical Findings." *Research in Accounting Measurement,* edited by Robert K. Jaedicke, Yuji Ijiri, and Oswald Nielsen. Evanston, Illinois: American Accounting Association, 1966.

[23] ――――――, ――――――, ――――――, ――――――. "Corporate Personality as Reflected in Accounting Decisions: Some Preliminary Findings." *Journal of Accounting Research,* Vol. 2, No. 2 (Autumn, 1964), pp. 183-96.

[24] Stedry, Andrew C. *Budget Control and Cost Behavior.* Englewood Cliffs, N.J.: Prentice-Hall, Inc., 1960.

[25] ――――――. "Budgeting and Employee Behavior: A Reply." *Journal of Business,* Vol. XXXVII, No. 2 (April, 1964), pp. 195-202.

[26] Vatter, William J. "Obstacles to the Specification of Accounting Principles." *Research in Accounting Measurement,* edited by Robert K. Jaedicke, Yuji Ijiri, and Oswald Nielsen. Evanston, Illinois: American Accounting Association, 1966.

[27] ――――――. "Postulates and Principles." *Journal of Accounting Research,* Vol. 1, No. 2 (Autumn, 1963), pp. 179-97.

THE BEHAVIOR OF "BEHAVIORAL" ACCOUNTANTS
CRITIQUE

William J. Bruns, Jr.

Professor Becker has neatly catalogued in his paper some early studies concerned with behavioral implications of accounting. In doing so he has provided an important service. He has contributed by offering expert opinion from outside the field of accounting on the work which some students of accounting have been attempting to do. He raises important criticisms that should be carefully considered in future work. However, I am disturbed by the implication that almost all work in behavioral accounting to date has been unfruitful. In fact, I believe we would be unprepared to accept his major recommendations if the work done to date had not been completed.

The major theme around which Becker builds his paper is simple to understand. He points out that accounting is potentially a discipline within the behavioral sciences; and he has concluded that to realize its potential, accounting should be based upon a theory which accountants should now begin building. The theory should be concerned with regularities and irregularities within the coding-receiving process. Recognizing that accountants code in different ways and receivers code in different ways and receive different amounts of information, Becker concludes that the accountant should be interested in how and why the coding-transmission-receiving system is modified.

In his review of accounting research, which can be said to have a behavioral science orientation, Becker emphasizes again and again that these studies fail to provide useful evidence because they were conducted without reference to underlying theory, they were poorly designed, and they had few controls. I am sure he feels able to support all of these allegations, and in many cases, perhaps no one could refute his conclusions. It is important to note, however, that the work which he criticizes has stimulated others to undertake similar and related studies, and without this increased interest the very recommendations that he makes would have little impact.

I wish I had time to speak in defense of the work that some of my friends have done and on which Becker has commented. I have no particular desire to defend my own work on which he has commented because those studies were done many years ago. At that time I was aware of some shortcomings, and time has allowed others to point out many more. Nevertheless, I think it may be important to note that some of the criticisms which Becker makes of my work and that of others seem overdrawn, and they reveal how difficult it is for a person expert in one field to become a knowledgeable commentator in another.

Consider, for example, my first study, which was begun in 1961, and which is the first that Becker discusses in his paper. In this study, a business game was used in a laboratory environment in an attempt to test whether or not different methods of inventory valuation would have systematic effects on operating decisions of managers in hypothetical business situations. Becker has apparently assumed that there is no theory to suggest differential effects or reasons for them. Had he read the original report of this study, he would have found references to its theoretical roots [2]. It is unfortunate that I was unable, in the published report of that research which Becker apparently did read, to spell out the source and nature of "inventory profits" which arise when FIFO valuation is used, and a rather elaborate theory of the impact of inventory valuation methods which I had developed, following in the footsteps of economists who had developed theories that suggested production quantities and prices might be affected by inventory accounting procedures. It is regrettable that I was unable to quote Henry B. Arthur, who wrote in *The American Economic Review* [1, p. 37] about the effects of conventional (FIFO, full absorption) procedures in 1938 and concluded that:

> . . . as soon as increasing or decreasing prices affect the value of commodities held in inventories, there is developed a chain of events which constitutes a powerful cumulative factor in the cyclical swings. . . . the individual business-man, believing that his inventory gains are real profits, is lead to extend his business on the basis of them. He may attempt to spend or distribute them . . . use them to expand his business, . . . or . . . he may bid up market prices still farther because the profitableness of the business has made a seller's market.

> . . . there can be no doubt that inventory gains lead to a false sense of optimism . . . little question but that such optimism leads to *mistaken judgments* and actions. . . . The false guides provided by the conventional income statement . . . help to carry business psychology to extremes. . . .

As a young graduate student, I read those words and accepted the argument as logical. Despite the fact that Arthur, and many others who wrote in the same vein, did not provide any empirical evidence to support their contentions that accounting information might have such dramatic effects, I based my theory on their assertions. The theory was naive, but it was a theory from which hypotheses were developed. When tests of the hypotheses proved negative or inconclusive, there seemed little reason to publish the entire theory. I assumed that most readers of my study would be familiar with the related earlier works. Perhaps I should feel embarrassed to reveal that I never considered the idea that a psychologist without extensive background in economics and accounting might read my work as carefully as Becker obviously has done.

As I said before, while I do not wish to speak in my own defense since I would never conduct the same study in the same way again anyway, I do wish to acknowledge that I know that the design of the studies noted was primitive. I know many ways in which they could be improved if they were replicated. Becker probably knows even more, and if I had known where to go for his help, I am sure that the original designs would have been different. Likewise, I am willing to acknowledge that the experimental controls were not strong, but I am not sure they were insufficient. To assert or imply that there were no controls in some of the studies cited is an extreme judgment.

In his discussion of the weaknesses of controls in studies and the failure to find evidence that *relevant* information for decisions, when varied, seemed not to affect the decisions, Becker seems to imply that the focus of these studies has been wholly on determining what effects would be and what they are in fact. I think some of them addressed a more basic issue, and that is, are those things that accountants have always felt were relevant considered so by decision makers? I have the feeling that Becker might be wondering, "What will be the effect if a rule for accounting is changed?" Whereas, I know many accountants are asking, "Does anybody read and use my report?" The latter question might be answered "yes," but decisions still might not vary with a change in accounting methods.

Having concluded that work done to date has little or no stated theoretical basis, has been poorly designed, and has for the most part been conducted with little or no control over experimental or field environments, Becker goes on to recommend that in the future these deficiencies be corrected. While I do believe that chance discoveries of significance could occur prior to development of theory, I do not believe anyone would wish to dispute such a conclusion, and I think all accountants could agree that future work should be better designed and more closely controlled than that which has been done in the past.

While we could all agree to try harder — to conduct only perfect studies — I am not so sure that we will meet with success in making future research in behavioral accounting look as neat and as conclusive as some research in psychology with which I am sure Becker is quite familiar.   In accounting, we are relatively newer at research than almost all other behavioral sciences.   We do not have a history of research, and our graduate programs do not always succeed completely in training students in research methods and methodology.   Likewise, I believe that many of the questions that must be answered are very complex.   Complex research often looks confused in the early stages.

I know that other behavioral scientists would agree that not all research is equally well designed and fruitful.   In a report of a four-week seminar held in 1958 including Leon Festinger, Wendell R. Garner, D. O. Hebb, Howard F. Hunt, Douglas H. Lawrence, Charles E. Osgood, B. F. Skinner, Donald W. Taylor, Michael Wertheimer, and invited consultants on research and research training in psychology, an attempt was made to describe the research process [3, p. 169]. Noting that over the years ". . . a stereotype has developed in the scientific as well as in the public mind as to what constitutes serious psychological research and scientific proof," the report summarized characteristics of that stereotype: "previous findings elaborated by . . . genius;" "crucial experiments;" "scientific rigor;" "all alterna- tive interpretations considered and accepted or rejected;" "confirmed discovery inserted into a systematized lattice of already available knowledge to complete for posterity a forward step, however small, toward man's mastery of the unknown."   The report continues:

> Make no mistake about it, however, this stereotype in name is a stereotype in fact, with all the over-simplification, mis-emphasis, and error which stereotypes involve.
> . . . .
> Actually, the process of doing research — that is, of creating and building a science of psychology — is a rather informal, often illogical and sometimes messy-looking affair.   It includes a great deal of floundering around in the empirical world, sometimes dignified by names like "pilot studies" and "exploratory research." Somewhere and somehow in the process of floundering, the research worker will get an idea. In fact, he will get many ideas. On largely intuitive grounds he will reject many of his ideas and will accept others as the basis for extended work. To make the picture even less amenable to rational understanding the ideas he accepts and cherishes and in which he invests his time and resources will sometimes even fly in the face of "known facts."
> . . . .
> It is in this sort of activity, rather far removed from the public, more orderly and systematic phases of scientific work, that the productive researcher spends much of his time and effort.   More- over, these activities must come first in time, else there is little new or worthwhile to process with the paraphernalia of confirmation. And, of course, the job is rarely, if ever, finished by doing one

experiment and finding a significant difference. Making a contribution of knowledge is a process of continuous work during which ideas change and develop. [3, p. 169].

I feel that in behavioral accounting we are all still in the very messy stage. If we are, then those of us who have done work in this field may have been premature in publishing our early findings, which have been largely the result of processes of groping and grappling with the issues that arise when one considers the impact of accounting on people, their decisions, and the organizations in which they work. On the other hand, publication has provided a means of sharing our thoughts, of interesting others in joining us, and of teaching our students something about how research problems are isolated. With Becker's help, we are now also better prepared to discuss some shortcomings of our work. It may also be that we have uncovered some new insights which we can use to develop a theory on which we can proceed.

Accounting will not realize its potential as a behavioral science until more people begin to work to develop our knowledge of the behavioral implications of accounting. Even if more people join the search, I have no illusion of quick and conclusive solutions to the problems of behavioral accounting. Assistance from other behavioral scientists will speed the search for solutions, particularly if they will explain the relevance of work that has been done in their disciplines to the accountant's tasks, his methods, and his procedures. I hope that other behavioral scientists will join Professor Becker in attempting to learn something about accounting and that they will not stop before they have learned enough to give us the kind of help that we need.

BIBLIOGRAPHY

[1] Arthur, Henry B. "Inventory Profits in the Business Cycle." *The American Economic Review,* Vol. XXVIII, No. 1 (March, 1938), pp. 27-40.

[2] Bruns, William J., Jr. "A Simulation Study of Alternative Methods of Inventory Valuation." Unpublished Ph.D. dissertation, University of California, Berkeley, 1962.

[3] Taylor, Donald W., et al. "Education for Research in Psychology." *The American Psychologist,* Vol. XIV, No. 4 (April, 1959), pp.167-79.

THE BEHAVIOR OF "BEHAVIORAL" ACCOUNTANTS

CRITIQUE

Andrew C. Stedry

Before commenting on the content of Professor Becker's paper, I want to emphasize the contrast between his paper and the colloquium paper of Professor Lazarsfeld. In the latter paper, Professor Lazarsfeld suggests that accountants should broaden their horizons to include social measurement. In essence, he implies accounting can indeed contribute to sociology. If I read Becker correctly, he takes the opposite point of view that we cannot contribute to accounting, much less to any other social science, unless we adopt the methodology developed in psychology in all of our dealings with behavioral variables. The possibility that research in accounting might contribute to psychology is not even considered by Becker. Thus, Lazarsfeld suggests that accountants should become involved in measurement problems of interest to sociologists, while Becker suggests that researchers in the behavioral aspects of accounting seek the aid of psychologists and other social scientists.

In fairness to Professor Becker, he was not invited to discuss the above mentioned issue; rather, he was asked to be one of several contributors to accounting thought from other disciplines, as indicated by the subtitle of this conference.[1] Apparently, the contribution from psychology must be stated almost entirely in negative terms. In his paper, Becker has examined "the behavior of 'behavioral' accountants" and found it wanting. With the possible exception of those studies in which he participated,[2] Becker provides, as the contribution from psychology, the broad-gauged condemnation of the attempts of a small but active group within the accounting discipline to introduce the tenets of psychology into the study of accounting. I agree entirely with the criticisms of the cited works, both alluded to and made explicit in the paper, present company excepted of course. But, alas, excepting present company would mean that I disagree with half of what he has said. The group of those researchers who have been addressing themselves to behavioral issues in accounting is pitifully small. I cannot

---

[1]Contributions to Accounting Thought by Other Disciplines.
[2]See [8] and [9].

believe that scathing attacks by a behavioral scientist, however justified, will serve to make this group larger.

Perhaps we can borrow some elementary concepts from the discipline of psychology in order to analyze the probable consequences of attacks by behavioral scientists. If an accountant chooses to apply psychological precepts to accounting, then he must pay a penalty. This penalty is the criticism of his methodology and the dismissal of his conclusions by someone recognized as an authority in psychology. The accountant learns to avoid this penalty because there are no corresponding rewards from the psychological authority. This lack of corresponding reward is illustrated in the paper (Becker's) under discussion. In short, the accountant will find more rewarding activities.

Let us now consider the content of this paper. Becker criticizes the admittedly loose and exploratory auditing field study made by Neil Churchill and William Cooper [5].   However, he ignores other relevant literature in his analysis. In particular, he fails to comment on the extremely tight, closely controlled laboratory study reported by the same authors on the behavioral effects of auditing records, reported a few months earlier [4, pp. 250-75]. This study escapes mention, being above reproach from the methodological standpoint, to the extent that any experiment based on a real problem can be above reproach.

The same sort of omission is made by Becker with respect to the work of William Bruns, Jr., as Bruns has pointed out already. Becker commented on an admittedly emasculated, published version of Bruns' early work [2] while ignoring the more complete description of the study [3]. We can ask why it was impossible to publish the report in its full form, and I think we may deserve appropriate criticism on that score.

There are more examples of Becker's selectivity. In particular, to my knowledge Becker has not made any comment about the field study which I did [6] on the behavioral effects of budgeting in conjunction with an experienced industrial psychologist, Emanuel Kay. This study was published in *Behavioral Science,* and included a full discussion of hypotheses, controls used, and other aspects of the study. With this type of selectivity, Becker seems to endeavor to throw the baby out with the bath water. Admittedly, the water is very, very dirty; but to borrow from psychology again, a young baby thrives on being nourished rather than slapped.

Presumably, the studies in which Professor Becker was involved are methodologically satisfactory.[3] Even so, I find the conclusion that keeping two sets of books is related to managerial personality is about as interesting as a good novel about, say, embezzlement.   Both are

_____
[3]See [1, pp. 167-80], [7, pp. 1-17], [8, pp. 200-210], and [9].

relevant, equally relevant, to the pressing questions facing accounting today.

The really pressing issues can be stated in the form of a single question: How do we change accounting so that it better satisfies the information demands of investors and managers in the world of today as well as the world of the future? I define information broadly here to include those aspects of information which cause the decision makers to act in certain ways upon the receipt of the information. The question encompasses such issues as: How do investors interpret accounting information and behave in response to accounting information? How should accounting be changed so as to provide investors with the capability for making better decisions, given that they behave as they do? How do operating supervisors respond to budgets and comparative performance reports? How should the latter be changed so that supervisors will behave in such a way that their welfare as well as that of the firm is enhanced? These, I think, are at least some of the pressing issues facing us in areas where behavioral science is relevant.

It is not sufficient to state that accountants should begin building theory and deducing testable hypotheses. I firmly wish that Professor Becker, having said this, would help us formulate relevant theory and testable hypotheses in the behavioral accounting area, rather than merely criticizing the methodology of those who are attempting, however ineptly, to engage in behavioral research.

I look forward to the possibility of cooperation between psychologists and accountants in theory building and hypothesis testing. As Bruns has already concluded, we can and should cooperate with behavioral scientists for the benefit of accounting theory. Hopefully, at some date in the future, accountants will become sufficiently sophisticated to contribute to the other behavioral sciences.

BIBLIOGRAPHY

[1] Archibald, T. Ross. "The Return to Straight-Line Depreciation: An Analysis of a Change in Accounting Method." *Empirical Research in Accounting: Selected Studies, 1967*. Chicago: The Institute of Professional Accounting, Graduate School of Business, University of Chicago, 1968.

[2] Bruns, William J., Jr. "Inventory Valuation and Management Decisions." *Accounting Review*, Vol. XL, No. 2 (April, 1965), pp. 345-57.

[3] —————. "Simulation Study of Alternative Methods of Inventory Valuation." Unpublished Ph.D. dissertation, University of California, Berkeley, October, 1962.

[4] Churchill, Neil C., and William W. Cooper. "Effects of Auditing Records: Individual Task Accomplishment and Organization Objectives." *New Perspective in Organizational Research*, edited by W. W. Cooper, H. J. Leavitt, and M. W. Shelly, II. New York: John Wiley and Sons, Inc., 1964.

[5] ——————, ——————. "A Field Study of Internal Auditing." *Accounting Review*, Vol. XL, No. 4 (October, 1965), pp. 767-81.

[6] Kay, Emanuel, and Andrew C. Stedry. "The Effects of Goal Difficulty on Performance: A Field Experiment." *Behavioral Science*, Vol. XI, No. 6 (November, 1966), pp. 459-71.

[7] Neumann, Frederick L. "The Auditing Standard of Consistency." *Empirical Research in Accounting: Selected Studies, 1968.* Chicago: The Institute of Professional Accounting, Graduate School of Business, University of Chicago, 1969.

[8] Sorter, George H., Selwyn W. Becker, T. Ross Archibald, and William H. Beaver. "Accounting and Financial Measures as Indicators of Corporate Personality — Some Empirical Findings." *Research in Accounting Measurement*, edited by Robert K. Jaedicke, Yuji Ijiri, and Oswald Nielsen. Evanston, Illinois: American Accounting Association, 1966.

[9] ——————, ——————, ——————, ——————. "Corporate Personality as Reflected in Accounting Decisions: Some Preliminary Findings." *Journal of Accounting Research*, Vol. 2, No. 2 (Autumn, 1964), pp. 183-96.

ACCOUNTING AND SOCIAL BOOKKEEPING*

Paul Lazarsfeld

PRELIMINARY CONSIDERATIONS

At the fringes of the boundaries of contemporary accounting theory and practice, there now exists a rapidly growing technology of measurement which includes an increasing area of our changing society as its scope of application. No study by a committee on the future of the accounting profession would be complete without some consideration of the emerging measurement area, even though it may be inappropriate or impossible to include such developments in accounting theory or practice.

FUTURE AREAS OF POSSIBLE ACCOUNTING PRACTICE

Operating under the general heading of Social Research (although it includes social bookkeeping as well), the development at the fringes of our discipline is of such scope and magnitude that complete acceptance of it as the nature of the accounting discipline would dwarf our current conception of the nature of the accounting function in society. It may be that this issue is not relevant to the current practice of the accounting function but that it will be an issue for consideration after 1975. Whether or not the development is pertinent to accounting practice in the near future, it is currently significant to educators and others concerned with the development of the future generation of accountants and to researchers concerned with the development of the accounting discipline.

*This paper was prepared by Norton M. Bedford. It is based on consultations with Paul L. Lazarsfeld in connection with the deliberations of the Long-Range Objectives Committee of the AICPA. Professor Lazarsfeld received permission to use this paper as the basis for his remarks at the Colloquium. It is published here with the kind permission of Professor Bedford and the Institute.

Broadly, the area involved covers the entire field of measurements useful for the operation of society. Business measurements, to which accounting is now closely tied, would represent only one part of the scope of the field. It would probably involve the use of measurement methods not now part of the accounting discipline. The profession capable of performing this function would contribute substantially to the development of both business individually and society in general. The activities performed by practicing members of such a broad profession could range from census taking to index number construction to governmental budgetary control; and the measurement methods used could vary from conventional quantitative procedures to ranking procedures to qualitative evaluations.

No precise boundaries now exist for the new field as it is still in a process of development. It is growing rapidly, however, and there are at least seven points where developments in the emerging area of social research now touch or come close to the accounting discipline. These points are as follows:

1. The attest function;
2. The budget function;
3. The problem of measurement;
4. The problem of conflict and collaboration;
5. The problem of training;
6. The research function;
7. The social measurement function.

THE ATTEST FUNCTION

The need for the attest function in society is growing. Not only is this true in the area of business, as every accountant knows, but in the social science area as well there are a lot of activities which need attesting. Social research has become big business and is engaged in such activities as television ratings and public opinion surveys, where sampling is used to collect information. When sampling is used to develop information, there is a need for objective verification and attesting that the sampling has been properly performed. It has long been possible to audit sampling procedures, and the techniques required are known to most CPAs who develop sampling procedures for financial audits, but accountants are not now typically assumed to be authorities in such areas. For example, a technical committee for the Congressional Committee investigating television ratings included no accountants. Apparently the basic competence of accountants in such an area is not recognized. Nor were accountants used in the Social Science Research Council's investigation of the 1948 incorrect prediction of the presidential election by public opinion polls. In both of these instances an attestation, or auditing, was needed regarding the adequacy of the sampling procedures. The function is now being performed in many other areas of social activity by social researchers and not CPAs.

THE BUDGET FUNCTION

The growth of applied science has created a vast area having involved budgetary problems. The government spends great sums on research grants and needs better budget estimates of the cost of proposed research projects if research is to be kept under control. Many cases may be cited to call attention to the need for research control. At the present time the budget estimates of such items as the cost of a supersonic airplane, the cost of new weapons of war, or any involved research project, are quite crude, and a need for improved budgeting exists. An article in the *Public Opinion Quarterly* titled "Social Research Dollars and Sense" [1] has pointed out that budgeting and auditing of scientific research projects is a completely new problem in our society. This is true for both physical and social science research. At the present time governments and foundations do not know how to budget research projects and they do not know how to audit research budgets submitted to them. For example, a project to simply find out the number of organizations in the country could be budgeted only crudely because there was no information indicating how the project should be carried out. Budgeting would involve breaking down such a project into the separate activities involved, i.e., determining the sample to use, preparing the questionnaire, conducting the interviews in the field, making the statistical analysis, and writing the reports, so that realistic cost estimates could be made. This procedure, while obvious to the CPA-trained mind, is not understood by many of those engaged in scientific research. The general principles of budgeting are completely unknown to them. Budgeting the use of a computer and the assignment of computer overhead costs are other illustrations of the budgetary problems involved in research projects which are now crudely measured by social researchers.

The auditing of research projects and research bureaus in terms of efficient performance is also an undeveloped area into which accountants could move. A type of auditing particularly needed in the research area at the present time is the evaluation of proper overhead charges to be included in governmental contracts and grants. No one knows the law on the assignment of overhead to projects and no one really knows what to do about charging overhead to research projects. There is a need for a CPA attestation of the proper over-head charge for research contracts and grants. Currently, researchers are acting as amateur accountants in this area and there is a great need for professional accountants. CPAs could perform a desirable service by acting as intermediaries between government and universi-ties or other research groups in cost determination and evaluation of research projects.

THE PROBLEM OF MEASUREMENT

Measurement methods have expanded substantially and there is no reason why an accountant should limit himself to those methods attached to some conventional definition of accounting. There are large new areas of measurement of performance and measurement of existing activities which accountants could invade if they knew about them. Although it would bring accountants into competition with social researchers and others, accountants could take all sys-tematic measurement into the province of their activities. Account-ing would then involve the planning of measurement, the attesting of measurement, and the checking or evaluation of measurement. It would involve accountants in a wide range of activities, even in-ternational affairs. New methods of measurement available to ac-countants in performing this broad function are discussed by Warren S. Torgerson in *Theory and Methods of Scaling* [3].

There are problems which the accounting profession will encounter when it enters the broader area of activity, not the least of which is the need for an understanding of each subject matter to be mea-sured, particularly in the planning of the measurement to be made and the information to be revealed. This need may require special-ization by accountants in different subject matters, over and above an increased competence in the measurement technology. Such specialization may involve additional problems in the training of profes-sional accountants, but the need for specialization nevertheless exists. In part, it has arisen as social research efforts have developed to the point where the need for social bookkeeping becomes an important part of organized society. For example, 200 years ago, the problem of the census was a research project dealing with such questions as how to sample and how do people answer. Now these research issues have been settled and the problems of the census have moved from the research level to the surveying or social bookkeeping activity. Similarly, the problem of computing unem-ployment in the country was a research problem forty years ago, dealing with such issues as the definition of an unemployed person.

Currently, the problem of computing unemployment is a counting process in the area of social bookkeeping.

It is when the measurement of various social information becomes routine that social research becomes social bookkeeping and the need for auditing and attesting arises. From this position it follows that specialization in subject matter becomes a problem of the profession. Social problems move continuously from research to social bookkeeping and the problem of the future practice of accounting and the training of young accountants becomes one of knowing the new areas of accounting measurements which will be needed in the future. In terms of a definition of the accounting function in society, acceptance of the broader area as part of the accounting function implies that the accounting profession deals with anything measured in some kind of repeated fashion. This does not mean that every accountant would have to know everything. Specialization would exist, but the totality of the profession should cover all fields where repetitive social measurements exist, including the new fields of social bookkeeping.

There is a common web that runs throughout all measurement regardless of the area in which the accountant is involved. Familiarity with this common body of knowledge of measurement would enable accountants with a limited amount of subject matter specialization to enter a variety of areas. For example, auditing the testing of a new pharmaceutical invention, dealing with questions of whether or not the company used enough cases and whether or not they matched applications in the test to results from the test — toward the objective of certifying as to the effectiveness of the new drug — could represent an important area of accounting activity. There are a great number of agencies in this country which collect and disseminate social science information and this is completely an accounting function which accountants could be doing.

Another problem the accounting profession will encounter when it enters the broader field of measurement is getting prospective users to accept and prefer accounting measurements, as opposed to the measurements of some other group, such as social researchers. The problem is particularly acute because nobody now thinks about seeking the services of an accountant to deal with such problems as governmental evaluation of requests for educational research grants or an educational board's efforts to allocate funds appropriately. There is still the accepted conception of the accountant, in his auditing capacity, as one who just checks up to see whether or not anybody has spent fifty cents where he was not supposed to spend it — a marginal and often unnecessary activity. It seems realistic to assume that, in the broader measurement activities, the accountant might well be only one of several measurement authorities and that the final decision on a proposed action would be decided collectively.   But the accountant needs to battle in this broader area to improve his general public image. And he needs to do battle in the new measurement areas because the problems of planning future activities, budgeting for them, and attesting as to their effectiveness are so complicated that no single person or group can make the decision. Society needs more measurement authorities as participants in these problems.

THE PROBLEM OF CONFLICT AND COLLABORATION

Every profession has the problem of conflict and collaboration. For example, accounting principles can either be in conflict with the tax law or they can collaborate with it. Or accounting concepts can be in conflict with economic or legal concepts or collaborate with them. Accountants may be in conflict with bookkeepers or in collaboration with them. When the profession expands its scope of activities, it may be either in conflict or it may collaborate with other fields.

In the field of social research, there are two areas where the profession will face the conflict or collaboration issue.   The first of these is the area of measurement of social organizations.   Will the accounting profession study the business enterprise in order to measure enterprise effectiveness only in terms of profit or loss or will it study the development of measurements of effectiveness in terms other than profit or loss, such as worker happiness or consumer satisfaction?   There are new types of measurement being developed which will allow the latter to be done to some degree. If the accountant does provide measurements in the broader area, he may find himself in conflict or collaboration with measurements by social researchers. Another example of a problem where the social researcher and the accountant could be in conflict or in collaboration would be in measuring the popularity of every published song or book. There is now no organized alternative measurement of the popularity of songs and books and there should be. This service is needed and no accountant now works on it.

The second area of possible conflict or collaboration between accounting and social research is in the use of the computer. The computer is invading all divisions of business and this raises the issue of who should control the computer. A power fight could develop between accountants and other groups, for the division which controls the computer also controls the investments of the company. The stakes are high in this conflict or collaboration issue, for the status and prestige of the various professions will be dependent upon the outcome.

THE PROBLEM OF TRAINING

The accountant and the social researcher are very much in the same predicament concerning the training area. They are both technicians and methodologists in fields which require specialized training. Business schools in principle do not train specialists. They train leaders and because this is the fashionable thing to do, they will not change. University psychology departments and sociology departments study rat behavior and the history of mankind to the extent that they do not develop specialized technicians and methodologists for social research measurements.

Although accounting and social research have developed in different camps, business and social science, the field of market research may be an area of overlap between the two professions. There is now no place in the university where young men are trained adequately to do market research. The type of market research study needed is not provided in the marketing departments of schools of business. This suggests the possibility of a specialized educational program suitable for both accountants and social researchers.

It is becoming clearer that the universities will have to develop a new professional school to train technicians and methodologists to perform the measurement function in society. Both accountants and social researchers could attend this school, and it would be as distinct a professional school as the journalism school, the medical school, and the engineering school. This school would need to have separate divisions because its graduates would go into different types of work. Each division might have its own specialized subjects to study after completing a core program. Accountants, whether or not they remain in the business school, could take certain courses in this professional school of measurement.

A number of universities are interested in developing the new professional school. Such a school could provide persons to aid the government on such problems as relocating West Virginia miners or evaluating the effect of the Voice of America in the Middle East. From the point of view of such a professional school, even the humanistically trained accountant would be only a special authority among many performing the function of measurement of human values, but the accountant would be necessarily a part of the whole problem of measuring values. The general problem with which the professional school would be inv lved is that of the applied human sciences, which is presently an American development alone.   Accounting is a specialty within the overall field.   The development of a professional school to train men for such a broad field follows the history of American education in that it is the result of combining parts of a variety of basic disciplines into an applied professional program. Such is the case of the school of journalism which no longer can be merely part of the English department.   Professional schools of social work combined parts of psychology and other disciplines for a distinct curriculum of their own.   Such is the nature and source of the emerging professional school of social measurement.   Within it might be a division of accounting, a division of market research, or any type of division dealing with organizational measurement, because it is a professional school which combines measurement with other aspects of human life and the life of society.   It is completely different from a school of business, for it ties measurement to philosophy, the social sciences, and to the humanities.   It will emerge, like every other professional school, by taking various traditional subject matter into a new combination for applied training. In operation, the professional school of social measurement might have a two year basic core followed by more specialized study in each particular division of study.

While there may be a tendency to assume accounting firms would not come to the professional school of social measurement in recruiting new employees, actually, the division of accountancy within the school should develop a curriculum which would be palatable in terms of contemporary uses of accountants.   These new young accountants would be equipped to perform both the contemporary accounting function and its enlarged function in the future.   Alternatively, a separate school of accountancy could be set up, initially tied closely to the school of business, but free to develop the accounting curriculum needed to prepare young men for the accounting function as it will exist in the future.

THE RESEARCH FUNCTION

Among other objectives, accounting research should be of such a nature as to improve the public image of accounting.   There are a number of research areas at the boundaries of the accounting discipline on which a limited number of accountants could conduct research which would add substantially to the public image of the profession.   Illustrative of this type of research is a "Survey of Specialized Information Services in the Social Sciences" conducted by the Bureau of Applied Social Research and the National Science Foundation which could just as well have been done by a firm of accountants or by a committee of accountants. The survey was very successful, and the accounting profession could just as well have received the prestige and income from the project. It would have associated accountants with social measurements. Although the survey included social bookkeeping aspects (finding out what exists), it dealt with accounting as well, in that a measured evaluation of the bookkeeping data was also developed by the questionnaire. The result of the survey is a catalog with a statistical summary and evaluation of social science information sources, which is considered to be a significant social contribution.

Another illustration of the type of social research which accountants could do and add to their public image is represented by a problem discussed at a conference at Yale, sponsored by UNESCO, and partially financed by the Ford Foundation. The problem was one of developing measurements of social attitudes in different countries on a comparative basis. The first problem was to collect information presently available, but no one knew if attitude studies on social problems had been made in other countries. Also, a system of information retrieval was needed. In fact, a retrieval system is sorely needed for all types of information. There is a need for a central coding system where all types of information are available and can be retrieved and analyzed on a computer. The information retrieval problem has become so large that it is becoming a major industry dealing with a variety of information needs ranging from such activities as supplying a doctor or a research chemist with a report on all publications on a particular topic or field to a host of other situations where information is needed. Accountants could improve their public image by working in the area of information retrieval. They have the basic training to perform this function, because information retrieval starts with a bookkeeping function and develops into an accounting function of evaluating and communicating appropriate data for specific needs.

In general, both social bookkeeping and social accounting are now playing a substantial role in business development, and accountants need to expand, particularly in the area of research activities, from economic bookkeeping and economic accounting into the social area in order to improve their public image. Only a very small number of accountants would need to do research in the social area to accomplish such an objective. The opportunity is there, for a new world of social measurements has developed, and accounting research should be conducted in this area.

In addition, the accounting profession needs to be introspective. A recent issue of *Daedalus* [2] contained sociological reports on the nature of the legal profession, the medical profession, the clergy, teachers, and other professions. A similar study of accounting on a more comprehensive basis would represent a desirable research activity. Such a study might be concerned with the following questions: From what type of persons are new CPAs recruited? What happens to sons of CPAs? Are new CPAs different from old CPAs? How many different types of CPAs do we have? What is the motivation which causes young men to enter the CPA profession? What do CPAs do in their leisure time? What do they read? Where did they go to school? The CPA profession may be a transitional profession, a means for family advancement from a low income group to a middle class group and above. For example, the CPA profession may be a means for a family to enter big business. Having no family connections, the father may enter the CPA profession and from this vantage point his son may enter big business. Research of this type would be of help in planning for the development of the profession.

Related to the problem of conflict within the profession, taxes vs. auditing, is the whole problem of comparability on which research is needed to bridge the gap between different areas of activity. Current efforts of the Accounting Principles Board deal with certain aspects of the comparability of accounting reports, but the basic problem of comparability is broader than the work of the Accounting Principles Board. It is concerned with the meaning of comparability and the type of significant comparisons which are desired. For example, accounting research on comparability would deal with such questions as the following: How are the accounting reports of different companies to be compared? How is comparability to be developed and when does it exist?

Within each profession, members may be grouped as high, middle, and low level members. The top level of doctors, for example, spend a great deal of time at conventions, whereas the low level doctor is mainly concerned with activities in his neighborhood. Activities of doctors at the middle level are a mixture of the high and the low.

The middle level professional, in all professions, may have more time to play golf or bridge than either the top or low level professional. The middle level professional tends to read more than the top or low level, but he reads more in terms of contemporary reading, such as the Book-of-the-Month Club reading, and does not devote his time to professional reading. These conclusions are significant to research for it means that research activity in accounting will have to be supported by the top level group in the Association. The low and middle levels of the profession have neither the interest nor the finances to support the needed research.

THE SOCIAL MEASUREMENT FUNCTION

There is a growing need for more social measurements in society. The population census revealing individual characteristics is an illustration of social measurement now widely performed, but there are many other social measurements which could be made and on which research is needed. For example, there has never been a social measurement in the form of a decennial "happiness census," but interest in the problem of social measurement has advanced to the point where there is now research being done, supported by funds from the National Institute of Mental Health, to determine whether or not an appropriate measure of happiness could be developed and whether or not it should be tried experimentally in certain communities. Other social measurements which need to be developed are measurements of college success and measurements of the "climate" of colleges. The whole field of social measurement offers great opportunities and it is growing rapidly. It may be appropriate for the accounting profession to finance a doctoral dissertation on the application of the new measurement methods in the social sciences to accounting.

The problem of motivating accountants to study and to apply social measurement methods to social issues is somewhat difficult because of the lack of direct and obvious financial rewards to be gained by such activities. Financial rewards are available in the attesting of sampling, ratings, and in the budgeting of research projects, but these rewards will probably be reaped by a limited number of accountants specializing in social measurement. As a result, the motivation needed to induce every young accountant to gain a minimum understanding of social measurements and the expansion of the measurement technology which goes with it will have to come from other motivations. The suggestion that the additional knowledge will pay off in an indirect way will serve as sufficient motivation for some. For others, the higher status which knowledge of social measurements will provide for the profession will be sufficient motivation. But the problem will be difficult, for like all professions, CPAs are not a completely homogeneous group of people. It may be that a substantial minority of the profession will never become competent in the social measurement field.

If accounting is the measurement profession in society, it would encompass social measurements within its scope. The problem is, however, that the measurement function is broader than business, and accounting has been defined as the "language of business" and even as the "profession of business." Despite the limitation implied by these definitions of accounting, there is no substantive reason why accountants should not compete in the future with mathematicians, statisticians, and social economists in the measurement field. This does not mean that the accountant would be merely a technician, for evaluation is also part of measurement; and it does not mean that accountants will ever be as competent as a creative statistician. Nor does it mean that accounting measurement must include all measurements in the social research area. But it does indicate that a general field does exist into which accounting, using its own terminology, could move in the future.

Whether accounting is more oriented to business or to measurement is not a settled issue on the side of business. A study of business under the title "The Social Sciences in Business" was completed without contact with accounting. Many students of business never mention the accountant or the auditor. Also, accounting is now used in many nonbusiness situations. In a sense, accounting may represent a measurement discipline having its greatest application in the business area but there is no reason to assume it will have to be contained to that area. As a measurement discipline, accounting may represent that body of knowledge required to perform the standard measurements in society. While the first development of a measurement may represent high-level research measurements, the second and subsequent times the measurement is made, it may represent accounting. This does not mean that accounting would be low-level technical work. To the contrary, in the expanded role, accounting could be a very high-level measurement function. Judgment would still be needed to decide how and what to measure.

THE SOCIAL ENVIRONMENT OF THE FUTURE

In addition to the rapidly developing role of measurement in society, which appears to be an important aspect of the future social environment in which accounting will operate, sociological findings suggest that the motivational values of society in the future may shift toward intellectual matters. Money may not be as strong a motivational value as it has been in the past. The intellectual aspects of accounting may become very esteemed by the young accountant of the future.

Another possible value development, in the realm of possible future values of society, may be that of contributing to the organization with which one is associated: whether that organization is a person's place of employment, his local, state, or national government, society in general, or any organization. It may well be that in the future it will be more important to contribute to society than it has been in times past. In any event, the rugged individualism of the businessman is disappearing rather quickly. But business remains the vital center of individualism both in creed and in practice, while the professions have greater concern with the community interest. However, business is becoming more professionalized; therefore, a more complete and harmonious reconciliation of individual and community interest may develop in the future.

THE SOCIOLOGY OF A PROFESSION

Sociologists, more than any other group, have studied professions. Some of their findings on the nature of a profession may suggest directions, means, or areas in which accountancy could develop in the future as it advances to a higher and higher professional level.[1]

A. There are four essential attributes of professional behavior:

    1. A profession rests on a high degree of generalized and systematic knowledge.

    2. A profession has a primary orientation to the community interest rather than to individual self-interest. Individual self-interest is not utterly neglected, of course, but it is served indirectly.

    3. A profession has a high degree of control over members through codes of ethics and through voluntary associations of members.

    4. A profession has a system of rewards (monetary and honorary) for occupational performance which are ends in themselves and not means to some end of individual self-interest.

B. The well-established professions have professional schools within universities that have a responsibility for developing new and better knowledge on which professional practice can be based, see to the ethical training of its students as well as to their other learning, and often grant awards to practicing professionals for exceptional performance for the profession.

C. Emerging professions depend heavily on leaders who take the initiative in pushing for the advancement of professionalism and in claiming public recognition for their profession. These leaders take, among others, the following actions:

    1. They construct and publish a code of ethics.

    2. They strengthen the professional association to carry on the functions of control and education of members, to communicate with the public, and to defend the profession against infringement by other groups.

---

[1]The following material is drawn from Bernard Barber, "Some Problems in the Sociology of the Professions," in [2, pp. 669-88].

3. They establish titles of more or less professional behavior, "hoping for example, to use such prestigious titles as 'fellow' as an incentive for the less professional to become more so."

4. They strengthen university professional schools.

D. In the area of politics, a profession is included among the list of "pressure groups" on the government.

E. The role of the professional in our society is becoming a more and more important feature of our kind of society.

BIBLIOGRAPHY

[1] Brunner, Edmund de S. "Social Research Dollars and Sense." *Public Opinion Quarterly,* Vol. XXVI, No. 1 (Spring, 1962), pp. 97-102.

[2] *Daedalus,* Vol. XCII, No. 4 (Fall, 1963), pp. 647-860.

[3] Torgerson, Warren S. *Theory and Methods of Scaling.* New York: John Wiley & Sons, Inc., 1958.

FINANCIAL FAILURE AND INFORMATIONAL DECOMPOSITION MEASURES

Baruch Lev

INTRODUCTION

A set of measures for the analysis of financial statements of firms was recently advanced by Henri Theil [8]. The measures, based on information theory concepts, were applied to financial statement decompositions (e.g., the decomposition of total assets to current and fixed) to describe the development of the decomposed items over time. A proportional development of these items (i.e., no change over time in their relative shares) was taken as a norm and measures were designed to indicate the extent of actual deviation from proportionality. Thus, informational measures indicate the degree of stability over time in financial statement decompositions.[1] The major difference between the informational analysis and the conventional ratio analysis is that the former focuses on the decomposition of a financial statement, i.e., on the relationships *within* a set of items, whereas the latter is usually applied to individual items, e.g., net income over total assets. The informational approach to financial statement analysis, therefore, seems to add a new dimension to the conventional analysis.

Although the suggested measures seem promising, their usefulness to financial statement users has not yet been tested. The measures would be regarded as useful if they can be incorporated in models designed to predict important business events (e.g., bankruptcies, mergers, etc.). Therefore, the first step in determining usefulness involves the study of the relationships between informational measures and such business events. This paper reports a test in which information measures were found to be associated with financial failure (bankruptcy) of corporations. The results indicate that the measures tested discriminate[2] between failing and nonfailing firms at least

---

[1]The question whether stability is desirable or not can be answered only with reference to specific business events, such as the one discussed in this paper, i.e., bankruptcy.

[2]Discrimination, here as elsewhere in the paper, does not mean perfect discrimination.

102

as far as five years prior to failure, and therefore may be usefully incorporated in models designed to predict financial failure.

TEST PROCEDURES

The sample for this study is comprised of 74 firms, 37 firms that failed and 37 that did not fail.[3]   Each failed firm in the sample is paired with a nonfailed mate of similar industrial classification, asset size, and financial statement dates.   The industry and asset size stratification is aimed at offsetting any effects related to the specific industry and asset size that might blur the possible relationship between information measures and the event of failure.[4] The paired analysis therefore allows a meaningful comparison between measures of a failed firm and those of its nonfailed mate.

Financial statement data of the failed firms were available for five years prior to failure.[5]   The first year before failure is defined as the year of the most recent financial statement prior to the failure date.   For example, if a firm failed in 1964 and its most recent financial statement was prepared for December 31, 1963, the first year before failure (year 1) would be 1963.   The fifth year before failure (year 5) would be 1959.   Financial statement data for the nonfailed firms correspond to the years that were assigned to their failed mates.

The following information measures[6] were computed for the balance sheets of the firms in the sample:[7]

Assets information measure. − This measure is of the form:

$$\sum_{i=1}^{2} q_i \log_e \frac{q_i}{p_i}, \text{ where}$$

q_1 and q_2 are the *fractions* of current assets and fixed assets, each divided by total assets. p_1 and p_2 are the corresponding fractions

---

[3]The data were kindly furnished by William Beaver. For a detailed discussion of the sampling methods see [3, pp. 72-8].

[4]For example, such an effect was reported by Alexander [1] who found that the rate of return to the firm will become more stable as asset size increases.

[5]Beaver's sample includes firms with data for less than five years. Our sample is restricted to firms with five-year data and is therefore smaller than the original.

[6]For a detailed discussion and examples of these measures see [8, Sections 3 and 7].

[7]Only balance sheet measures were tested because income statement data were not sufficiently detailed.

of an *earlier* balance sheet (e.g., q_1 and p_1 are the current assets fractions in 1968 and 1967, respectively).[8]

Liabilities information measure. — This measure is:

$$\sum_{i=1}^{3} q_i \log_e \frac{q_i}{p_i} \, , \text{ where}$$

q_1, q_2, and q_3 are the fractions of current liabilities, long-term liabilities, and equity, respectively, each divided by the balance sheet's total. p_1, p_2, and p_3 are the corresponding fractions of an earlier balance sheet.[9]

Balance sheet information measure. — This measure is of the form:

$$\sum_{i=1}^{2} \sum_{j=1}^{2} q_{ij} \log_e \frac{q_{ij}}{p_{ij}} \, , \text{ where:}$$

q_{11} is the fraction of current assets divided by twice the balance sheet's total,

q_{12} is the fraction of fixed assets divided by twice the balance sheet's total,

q_{21} is the fraction of current liabilities divided by twice the balance sheet's total,

q_{22} is the fraction of long-term liabilities (including equity divided by twice the balance sheet's total, and

p_{11} through p_{22} are the corresponding fractions of an earlier balance sheet.

The three informational measures describe the behavior of financial statement items (expressed as fractions of their total) over the time spanned by the two balance sheets. The measures will take a zero value when all corresponding items of the two balance sheets differ at most by a proportionality factor (i.e., $p_{ij} = q_{ij}$ for all i and j). The larger the discrepancy between corresponding fractions, the larger the measures. In essence, the informational analysis of financial statements takes a proportional development of items over time as a norm and indicates the degree to which the actual development of these items deviates from a proportional one.

---

[8]Current assets include cash, marketable securities, accounts receivable, inventory, and other current assets. Fixed assets include investments, net plant and equipment, other tangible noncurrent assets, and intangible noncurrent assets.

[9]Current liabilities include accounts payable, notes payable, and other current liabilities. Long-term liabilities include long-term debt, deferred taxes, other long-term liabilities, and preferred stock.

SUMMARY OF RESULTS

Five annual balance sheets were available for each firm in the sample. Applying an information measure to consecutive balance sheets (i.e., years 5 and 4, 4 and 3, 3 and 2, 2 and 1 prior to failure) results in four measures for each firm. Measures for a failed firm were then compared with corresponding measures of its nonfailed mate (e.g., the assets information measure of a failed firm for years 5 and 4 is compared with the assets information measure for years 5 and 4 of its nonfailed mate). This provides four individual comparisons for each pair of firms and 148 comparisons for the whole sample. Averaging the four measures for each firm results in one comparison per pair and 37 comparisons for each of the three information measures tested. Results of these comparisons are exhibited in Table 1 on page 106. A discussion of the findings follows.

The paired comparisons reported above indicate that information measures for the failed firms are larger than those for the nonfailed firms in more than 50 percent of the cases (70 percent for balance sheet information, 62 percent for assets information, and 66 percent for liabilities information). This result is even more pronounced when the consecutive measures for each firm are averaged (89 percent, 76 percent, and 73 percent). The average information measures over all firms (last two columns in Table 1) are substantially larger for the failed group than for the nonfailed one. These findings attest to the discriminating power of information measures with respect to financial failure. This discriminating power can be explained by noting that the measures indicate the stability of financial statement items over time. Failing firms usually undergo larger and more disproportionate changes in their assets and liabilities than nonfailing firms, as a result of the former's efforts to recover. One would therefore expect the financial statement items of failing firms to be less stable (and hence have larger information measures) than those of nonfailing firms.

The balance sheet information measure displays the greatest discriminating power of the measures tested (70 percent for individual comparisons, 89 percent for firms' averages). This might be explained by the fact that the balance sheet information measure captures all the changes that take place in assets and liabilities simultaneously.

The average measures over all firms show that liabilities information is larger than assets information for both failed and nonfailed firms. Yet this difference is much larger for the failed firms than for the nonfailed (.2098 vs. .0137 nits for the failed, .0115 vs. .0052 nits for the nonfailed). One can infer from this result that liabilities are less stable than assets for all firms, and that this difference is even larger for failing firms. This phenomenon is probably caused

TABLE 1

COMPARISON OF INFORMATION MEASURES FOR FIRMS IN THE SAMPLE

	Total number of comparisons	Number of cases in which $I_F > I_N$ [A]	Average information measures over all firms (in nits) [B]	
			Failed	Nonfailed
Balance sheet information:				
Consecutive years	148	103 (70%)	.0423	.0075
Firm's average over 5 years	37	33 (89%)		
Asset information:				
Consecutive years	148	92 (62%)	.0137	.0052
Firm's average over 5 years	37	28 (76%)		
Liabilities information:				
Consecutive years	140[C]	93 (66%)	.2098	.0115
Firm's average over 5 years	37	27 (73%)		

[A] I_F stands for the information measure of a failed firm, while I_N stands for the information measure of a nonfailed firm.
[B] The base of the logarithm in the information measures is usually left to the user's choice. When natural logarithms are used (as in this study) it is conventional in information theory to indicate the results as nits.
[C] In a few cases the comparisons were dropped since information measures cannot handle negative fractions [8, Section 9]. In these cases the equity of failed firms was negative. Thus, for the liabilities information measure we have only 140 comparisons.

by the instability of liabilities induced by the efforts of failing firms to reorganize and consolidate debts (including equities).

The information measures in Table 1 were applied to consecutive years only (i.e., years 5 and 4, 4 and 3, 3 and 2, 2 and 1 prior to failure). Measures were also applied to nonconsecutive years (e.g., years 5 and 1, 5 and 2, etc.). Results of this test for the balance sheet information measure are exhibited in Table 2.[10]

We note that the larger the interval between the two balance sheets, the larger the discriminating power of the measures (62 percent for a two-year interval, 65 percent for a three-year interval, and 76 percent for a four-year interval). The difference between the average measures over all firms (last two columns in Table 2) also increases with the time interval. These results are caused by the larger deviation from a proportional development of financial statement items as the time interval between balance sheets increases.

It is conceivable that balance sheets of fast growing firms also have large information values. In this case (for which there is no evidence yet), difficulties may be encountered in using information measures to discriminate between failing and very successful firms. This is not a serious limitation, however, since lenders may easily discriminate between the two extremes (i.e., very successful and

TABLE 2
COMPARISON OF BALANCE SHEET INFORMATION MEASURES FOR NONCONSECUTIVE YEARS

Years	Total number of comparisons	Number of cases in which $I_F > I_N$	Average information measures over all firms (in nits)	
			Failed	Nonfailed
5 and 3	37	23 (62%)	.0201	.0101
5 and 2	37	24 (65%)	.0452	.0149
5 and 1	37	28 (76%)	.1820	.0197

failing firms) by using other indicators (e.g., growth of share prices). The discrimination between failing and ordinary firms, for which information measures may be useful, is much more complicated.

---

[10]Results for the other two information measures follow exactly the same pattern and therefore are not reported.

Moreover, mistakenly identifying a successful firm as a failing one is considerably less serious to a lender than the reverse because of the different losses involved.   The loss from not granting a loan to a successful firm is the marginal interest rate charged to it (i.e., the difference between the firm's rate and earnings from comparable alternative investments).   On the other hand, the loss in granting a loan to a failing firm may involve capital as well as interest.

INFORMATION MEASURES AND FINANCIAL RATIOS

Financial ratios are extensively used by lenders to determine the solvency of a firm.   Users of these ratios argue that a firm is a reservoir of assets and its financial state is determined by the probability that this reservoir will be exhausted.   The probability of failure is therefore smaller when: a) the amount of total assets (especially, liquid assets) is larger, b) the amount of debt is smaller, and c) the flow from operations (income) is larger.   Ratios are used in this context to indicate the relative sizes of the asset reservoir, amount of liabilities, and flow from operations.[11]

It is instructive to compare the discriminating power of information measures (discussed in the preceding section) with that of financial ratios.   A simple comparison can be made by a dichotomous classification test in which the status of a firm is predicted solely on the basis of the measures.   Specifically, the two measures for a pair of firms (failed and comparable nonfailed) are examined and the failed firm is picked on the basis of the relative magnitude of the measures. For example, given the two balance sheet information measures for the pair, the one with the larger measure is picked as the failed firm; or, on the basis of the two working capital ratios (current assets over current liabilities) we choose the one with the smaller ratio as the failed firm.   Comparison of the predicted status of the firm with the actual status, over the whole sample, yields an error percentage (percentage of firms misclassified) which indicates the discriminating power of the measure.

Several representative ratios were chosen from the large number of possible ratios.[12]   They were computed for the firms in the sample and averaged over the five years to obtain a long-run measure.   The classification test was then applied and the percentage of error determined for each measure.   Results are exhibited in Table 3.

---

[11]For a detailed discussion with respect to financial failure see [3, pp. 79–80], and [9].

[12]These ratios represent the "traditional" categories in ratio analysis: balance sheet ratios (liquidity and solvency), income statement ratios (profit margin), and mixed ratios (capital turnover).   The choice of a specific ratio within a category is not of great importance since such ratios were found to be highly intercorrelated; see [6, pp. 48-49].

TABLE 3
PERCENTAGE OF ERROR IN THE DICHOTOMOUS
CLASSIFICATION TEST

Measure	Percentage Error
Balance sheet information	11 (4)[A]
Current assets / Current liabilities	27 (10)
Quick assets / Current liabilities	32 (12)
Current liabilities / Total assets	27 (10)
Total liabilities / Total assets	19 (7)
Quick assets / Total assets	49 (18)
Current assets / Total assets	46 (17)
Working capital / Total assets	16 (6)
Cash flow / Sales	11 (4)
Working capital / Sales	35 (13)
Total assets / Sales	30 (11)
Cash flow / Total debt	5 (2)
Cash flow / Net worth	24 (9)
Net income / Net worth	24 (9)

[A] Number of firms misclassified out of a total of 37 pairs.

The data in Table 3 show that only one ratio (cash flow to total debt) outperformed the balance sheet information measure in the classification test. This single exception is slight (a difference of only two firms misclassified) and probably of minor consequence. Note, however, that the information measures, due to data limitations, were calculated from balance sheet data only.[13] It therefore seems more meaningful to compare their performance with that of balance sheet ratios only (first 7 ratios in Table 3). Such a comparison indicates that the discriminating power of the balance sheet information measure is substantially superior to that of balance sheet ratios.

CONCLUDING REMARKS

Information theory suggests a set of measures for financial statement analysis. A preliminary test of the usefulness of these measures to financial statement users indicates that they can discriminate between failing and nonfailing firms and therefore may be incorporated in models designed to predict financial failure. It is also shown that an information measure outperforms many ratios currently used by financial analysts.

It should be noted, however, that the main objective of this study is to present initial evidence as to the possible usefulness of the new information measures and not to predict financial failure. Several studies [2, 7] showed that such a prediction can best be done in a multivariate framework rather than by using individual measures one at a time. Our results are therefore restrictive yet they suggest some opportunities for future research.

1. Information measures should be added to existing models designed to predict financial failure to examine the possible improvement in the performances of such models.

2. Several important business events were found in other studies to be associated with financial failure. For example, Hickman [5] reports that bond ratings published by rating agencies (e.g., the scale of nine rates from AAA through C published by Standard and Poor) are inversely related to the rate of bond failure. It is therefore possible that information measures are associated with these events and could be used to predict them.[14]

---

[13]See footnote 7.

[14]Another interesting event that is probably associated with financial failure (and hence with information measures) is the risk premium on corporate bonds; see [4].

BIBLIOGRAPHY

[1] Alexander, Sidney S. "The Effect of Size of Manufacturing Corporations on the Distribution of the Rate of Return." *Review of Economics and Statistics,* Vol. XXXI, No. 3 (August, 1949), pp. 229-35.

[2] Altman, Edward I. "Financial Ratios, Discriminant Analysis and the Prediction of Corporate Bankruptcy." *Journal of Finance,* Vol. XXIII, No. 4 (September, 1968), pp. 589-609.

[3] Beaver, William H. "Financial Ratios as Predictors of Failure." *Empirical Research in Accounting: Selected Studies, 1966.* Chicago: The Institute of Professional Accounting, Graduate School of Business, University of Chicago, 1967.

[4] Fisher, Lawrence. "Determinants of Risk Premium on Corporate Bonds." *Journal of Political Economy,* Vol. LXVII, No. 3 (June, 1959), pp. 217-37.

[5] Hickman, W. Braddock. *Corporate Bond Quality and the Investor Experience.* Princeton: Princeton University Press, 1958.

[6] Horrigan, James O. "The Determination of Long-Term Credit Standing with Financial Ratios." *Empirical Research in Accounting: Selected Studies, 1966.* Chicago: The Institute of Professional Accounting, Graduate School of Business, University of Chicago, 1967.

[7] Myers, James H., and Edward W. Forgy. "Development of Numerical Credit Evaluation Systems." *Journal of American Statistical Association,* Vol. LVIII, No. 303 (September, 1963), pp. 799-806.

[8] Theil, Henri. "On the Use of Information Theory Concepts in the Analysis of Financial Statements." *Management Science,* Vol. XV, No. 9 (May, 1969), pp. 459-80.

[9] Walter, James E. "The Determination of Technical Solvency." *Journal of Business,* Vol. XXX, No. 1 (January, 1957), pp. 30-43.

PART III

Problems in the Implementation of Accounting Research

INFLATION AND THE LAG IN ACCOUNTING PRACTICE

Solomon Fabricant*

INTRODUCTION

THE ACCOUNTING PROBLEM POSED BY INFLATION

Our era has aptly been called one of inflation. The general price level has been trending upward in the United States for almost a quarter of a century — even longer if we include the World War II period. While the rate of increase in this country has been less than in most other countries, it has not been negligible. Two or even three percent per annum may not look like much to some people, but these are compound-interest rates. Even over the few years that have elapsed since the American Institute of Certified Public Accountants [1] published its research study on *Reporting the Financial Effects of Price-Level Changes,* in 1963, the general price level has risen by 15 or 20 percent; and it is now (April, 1969) almost 60 percent above what it was in 1948 when the Institute set up its Study Group on Business Income [26].

Further, the rate of increase has been accelerating in recent years. As we all know, this has stimulated efforts now under way to stop the acceleration and then slow down the rate of inflation. The obstacles to be overcome are serious, however. No knowledgeable

*This is a revised version of the paper read at the Colloquium. Sections were added on "The Problem of Fixed Dollar Payments" and "Liberalized Depreciation Practices: An Offset?"

The paper is based on a section of a study of inflation under way at the National Bureau of Economic Research with the support of the Alfred P. Sloan Foundation. Because the paper has not gone through the Bureau's usual review procedure, it is offered on the responsibility of the author alone.

The National Income Division of the Department of Commerce kindly made available a number of unpublished series. Grateful acknowledgement is also made to Milton Friedman and Anna J. Schwartz, for access to some of their unpublished data; Chantal Dubrin, for taking charge of the calculations and for other assistance; Mildred Courtney, for valuable secretarial help; and H. Irving Forman, for the charts. For helpful comments on the first draft of the paper, I am obligated to Philip Cagan, Robert E. Lipsey, John R. Meyer, and Lee J. Seidler.

person expects, nor does the new Administration promise, a quick victory. But even if the current inflation should be brought to a halt within the next two or three years, it is very unlikely that there will be a return to earlier price levels. The effects of the inflation that we have already experienced will persist long after inflation is stopped. And there are some grounds for wondering whether any halt imposed on inflation will be permanent.

Surely, under these circumstances, one may ask whether it is not anachronistic, or at least incongruous, that the financial reports being issued by companies seldom breathe a word about the effects of changes in price levels on their carefully compiled and audited figures. No labor union fails to mention the consumer price index when engaged in a wage negotiation. Yet companies may report "record profits" and say nothing about the contribution of an attenuated dollar to these record highs. Only when profits decline may there be a reference to price increases, and then only to higher labor and material prices. Accounting practice has not yet been adjusted to the fact of inflation.

I hasten to add (we economists live in glass houses, just like other human beings) that the national accounts drawn up by economists are in some respects also deficient in taking account of general price changes, and I will have a word to say about this later. But these deficiencies are far less serious. Not even the most backward country today presents its estimates of Gross National Product without an accompanying set of estimates in "constant prices," if there is even the slightest basis on which to make the deflation.

THREE MAIN QUESTIONS

When the general price level is changing at a rate that may not be called negligible, to ignore its changes in the accounting reports that go to businessmen, investors, government officials, and others, can introduce significant error in their decisions and policies. Measurements of income and income distributions and the assessment of alternative investment opportunities, among other calculations, must inevitably be less accurate. And the imposition of taxes, for example, must be less equitable or otherwise fall short of attaining desired objectives. The accounts need to be adjusted in order to make more accurate the calculations on which public and private decisions and policies are based. Just how to do so is our first main question.

While I have already ventured the judgment that the miscalculations resulting from neglect of inflation are important, this judgment needs to be supported by evidence. At this point of the paper, I may claim only that the errors *can* be important. To show that the errors are in fact important, we must answer two other questions. We need to know, first, the degree of inaccuracy of various comparisons of profits and other accounting estimates over time, and also over space—for example, comparisons between industries and firms. Second, we need to know to what extent users of inaccurate accounts are in fact misled by the errors.

Economists have been worrying about these matters for a long time. One reason is their concern with the quality of the numerical data at their disposal. Another is their interest in economic behavior—in the present case, under the impact of inflation. Accountants also have been talking for decades about the problem of adjusting accounting records to changes in general price levels. But accountants seem to have done little more than talk, at any rate in the United States, where corporate reports generally neglect the problem, as I have already complained. Undoubtedly, among the factors that have given pause to accountants (and their clients) is the belief that the benefits to be derived from reporting on price-level changes would fall short of the costs. Maybe they are right. The information submitted below should help to resolve the question.

I shall add little that is new to what has already been said on the first question; i.e., how to adjust the accounts when price levels change significantly. But what has been said over the years has not been altogether consistent. There continue to be rather wide differences of opinion among accountants, and to a lesser extent also among economists, on the issues involved. Presentation, and hopefully clarification, of a consistent position and of the grounds on which it rests, may therefore be worthwhile. On the second question, the difference it would make in the figures, some added light is thrown by calculations recently made by economists working on the national income and on rates of return on business investment. The third question, whether and to what degree any or many people are misled by the unadjusted accounts, is in some respects the most interesting of the questions. It is certainly the most difficult, and one to which an answer can as yet be little more than speculative. But more work is needed on all three questions—work by accountants, by economists, and by both together. The discussion in this Colloquium will, I hope, serve to move us another step forward.

ADJUSTMENTS FOR CHANGES IN THE GENERAL PRICE LEVEL

CONVERSION TO A "STABLE DOLLAR"

To answer the question of how to adjust accounting data for changes in the general price level, we must be quite clear on what we are after. We want to make valid and useful comparisons of incomes, capital, and rates of return between different accounting periods and between different companies.

Valid comparisons require, first of all, a stable monetary unit — money adjusted not only for coin clipping, to hark back to olden times, but for any depreciation (or appreciation) of its value. The money unit would be stable, and the comparison valid for some purposes, if adjustments were made merely for changes in the value of the money in terms of gold, or silver, or any other generally acceptable single commodity. This was the adjustment of medieval times when currencies not fixed in terms of gold or silver were related to an "imaginary" or "ghost" money that was so fixed.[1] They were imaginary or ghostly, it hardly needs to be said, because no currency was able to survive the rigors of life in those days and remain stable in terms of gold or silver — any more than have the currencies of our own times. The conversion could, of course, be to another — an existent — currency that is stable, or relatively stable, in terms of gold. This is the kind of adjustment made now when calculations involving unstable currencies are converted to dollars.

An improvement over these simple methods of stabilizing the monetary unit is an adjustment that fixes the monetary unit in terms of its purchasing power over a wide range of goods and services, not just one of these. This idea came with the "tabular standard" of value suggested well over a century ago — one of a number of "rules for the guidance of mankind," as an early proponent put it — and later was made practical by the development of index numbers of prices. For most purposes the more useful, as well as stable, monetary unit is one that can purchase a fixed quantity — a "basket" — of the combination of all the goods and services (or a representative sample of all the goods and services) that are bought with money income, not a fixed quantity of just one or some of the goods and services. The value of the dollar, then, is to be fixed by correcting it for changes in the *general* price level.[2]

There are three price indexes, among those available currently, that may be regarded as indexes of the general price level — the GNP Implicit Price Index (IPI), the Consumer Price Index (CPI), and the Wholesale Price Index (WPI). The one that covers the full range of goods and services on which the national income is spent is the IPI. It is by no means perfect, as we shall see, but for our purpose it is the best there is, and it is good enough.

---

[1] Accountants were reminded of the purpose of "imaginary money," a few years ago, by Maurice Moonitz [21, pp. 19-20].

[2] John Maynard Keynes [19, Book II] provided what is still one of the best discussions of the problem of defining and measuring "the value of money."

Different groups buy somewhat different baskets of goods and services and make their purchases in different places. The purchasing power of a dollar of income received in different sectors of the economy therefore may (and to some degree does) rise more or less than the national average. This has been bothering economists, and they have asked whether it would not be appropriate, at any rate in principle, to use special indexes of prices tailored to the particular groups concerned — one index for Industry or Region or Income Class A, another for B, and so on. To this question, their answer has usually been "yes." When real incomes and changes in real incomes in Alaska in the early 1900's are to be compared with corresponding incomes and changes in incomes on the West Coast, a somewhat different price deflator for Alaska than for the State of Washington is required, and allowances must be made also for regional differences in price levels. The example is extreme, but it illustrates the general fact that anyone choosing between two places in which to live and work has to take two different price levels into account.

Our purpose, however, is to construct a stable dollar that is free of the effects of *general* price inflation or deflation. We do not want to be in the position of saying that inflation is raising the price level in Region A and deflation is reducing the price level in Region B, when the national price level is steady. The differential in the price movements between Region A and Region B is largely a reflection of relative price change, which we will discuss below, not of the inflation or deflation that is measured by changes in the general price level of the nation as a whole. It is the latter that is our present concern.

Apart from this consideration, there is another and compelling one. We need an adjusted dollar that can be used to make generally valid comparisons between many different times and places within the country. No single adjusted dollar will quite do for all of these comparisons, because of regional and other differences in price levels within the country. But it is far more convenient than a collection of many different specially adjusted dollars. The problem is, of course, the same problem, though less serious, that confronts economists when they make comparisons of the real incomes or purchasing powers of the currencies of many different countries. They have generally settled for a limited number of adjusted currencies.[3] When interest is primarily in adjusting the accounts of widely-held companies, doing a national business, adjustment of the dollar by means of a national general price index will suffice.[4]

---

[3]A recent example is provided by Braithwaite [2].

[4]We do not escape all dilemmas even for this purpose, however. When making a comparison between two dates in the same country, one must choose between the Paache and the Laspeyres price indexes, or use some rather arbitrary combination of the two. The quantitative difference between the two is usually, but not always, small.

CORRECTION FOR PRICE LEVEL "HETERO-TEMPORALITY"

To deflate accounting profits, as these are ordinarily calculated, by an index of the general price level would go a long way towards establishing comparability between the profits of different periods. But it would not go quite far enough. The reason is that the calculations in any accounting period are not entirely in terms of the current price level. They are partly in terms of the price levels of earlier periods as well, because some of the currently-charged costs (depreciation charges, for example) were incurred or contracted for in earlier periods and therefore at price levels different from the current price level. An adjustment is needed to express all costs charged during a period in terms of the price level of that period [7, 8]. Once this is done, the adjusted series of current-price incomes in successive periods can then be further adjusted to express them in terms of the price level of some single base period. This may be the most recent period, or an earlier one. It matters little which base is used, as long as it is the same for all the periods being compared. If the first step is omitted, however, the second step will not bring us quite to our goal.

This may be seen perhaps more clearly, if we imagine a situation in which the general price level and the level of prices of capital goods are moving up together and at a constant rate, and the stock of capital assets is stable in volume and composition. In this case, depreciation charges calculated at historical cost will always be less than depreciation at current replacement cost by an amount that depends on the rate of increase in the price level and the average difference between the year of acquisition of capital assets and the current year. Under the assumptions made, this difference will be equal to one-half the average length of life. Profits in each period, expressed in terms of the period's own current prices, will then be overstated by a constant fraction. The adjustment for hetero-temporality is intended to correct this overstatement. In addition, of course, the profits reported in successive periods will not be comparable to one another because they are expressed in dollars of different purchasing powers. The rates of change of profits between consecutive periods will be overstated by a constant amount, equal to the rate of change of the general price level. The adjustment for hetero-temporality corrects the *level* of reported profits. The conversion to constant prices corrects the *rate of change* (or slope) of reported profits.

An adjustment for hetero-temporality is also needed to make comparisons of rates of return, such as profits as a percentage of net worth, more valid than they would otherwise be. Were the numerators of these ratios, as given in income accounts, influenced by changes in the general price level to the same degree as the denominators given in reported balance sheets, there would be no need to adjust the ratios. But the timing of the effects on the two changes in the general price level is different. In any particular year, the prices implicit in the income account will, we may expect, reflect current prices more closely than will the balance sheet. The numerator of the rate of return ratio will therefore be subject to less correction, as a rule, than the denominator, and the rate of return will be overstated during inflation and understated during deflation. The degree of distortion in successive time periods will be similar, and therefore errors in making comparisons over time will be small, only if the rate of change of the general price level is approximately constant.

In addition to making comparisons between periods, we want to make valid and useful comparisons of income and rates of return of different firms or other economic entities in a given accounting period. The adjustment for heterogeneity of price levels within a period is necessary for this purpose also. Were the mix of price levels the same in all companies, the figures of all would be biased in the same direction and degree. In proportion to one another, then, the figures would be comparable. But the mix does vary from one company to another, because of variation in the composition and rate of turnover of assets, in the average age or year of acquisition of assets, and so on [17, 9]. This implies that the adjustments need to be tailored to the particular situation of each of the companies involved in a close comparison.

THE TREATMENT OF RELATIVE PRICE CHANGES

When material consumption and depreciation charges are calculated in terms of replacement costs, one of the two adjustments we want is thereby made. But one that we do not want is also thereby made.

To be more specific, replacement cost accounting in effect involves, first, the adjustment for hetero-temporality that we have just been discussing. The accounts of each period are expressed in terms of the period's own (homogeneous) general price level, a desirable step in adjusting the accounts for changes in the general price level. Second, however, replacement cost accounting involves also an adjustment that we do not want. This is an adjustment for changes in relative prices. Third, replacement cost accounting also fails to express the accounts of different periods in terms of the same general price level —an essential step in dealing with general price-level changes. The last is the most important failing, but it needs no discussion beyond what we have already given it. The treatment of relative price changes does require a further word. This is rather surprising because the distinction between adjustments for changes in the general price level and adjustments for changes in relative prices was made quite clear in *Accounting Research Study No. 6* [1, pp. 29–31]. However, there continues to be some confusion on the validity and significance of the distinction.

Changes in the general price level and changes in relative prices are not entirely unrelated, it is true. Some changes in relative prices take place for the same reason as changes in the general price level. Not all elements of the price system respond with equal promptitude or in equal degree to changes in money supply, for example. But most changes in relative prices occur apart from changes in the general price level. The two are influenced by largely separate and independent forces and can and should be dealt with separately.

Adjustment of accounting calculations of income for inflation or deflation — that is, for changes in the general price level — is not intended to eliminate the effects of change in relative prices. Indeed, the latter effects should not be eliminated if income is to be reported correctly, either in constant or in current prices.

To sharpen the distinction between the general price level and individual prices, consider a situation in which the general price level is stable. This does not mean that individual price levels, the average of which we call the general price level, are also stable. Changes in the weather, technological changes, depletion of subsoil assets, pressure of population on available land, and shifts in demand — all these make for increases in some prices and decreases in others. Few individual prices actually remain stable over any length of time. As was recognized in the price "guideposts" of the Kennedy and Johnson administrations, a policy designed to maintain a constant general price level must allow for changes in relative prices because productivity in different industries moves up at different rates [11, Chapter XI]. When the general price level is stable, it is because rising individual prices are being balanced by declining individual prices.

These differential price movements tend to produce gains that businessmen seek to make or losses they seek to avoid. The gains or losses resulting from differential price movements are part and parcel of the profits of business activity. While these gains or losses need to be expressed in dollars of constant purchasing power, if comparisons over time or space are to be valid, they do not need to be, nor should they be, eliminated when we adjust the accounts for changes in general price levels.[5]

---

[5]That differential price movements make for "real" profits or losses can hardly be gainsaid. The questions, rather, are: (1) whether to treat the effects of differential price movements

The point is quite general. It applies to the income of a worker, a company, an industry, or a nation. Thus, the real income of a nation may be said to depend on three things: the volume of resources it puts into production, the product it gets per unit of resources, and the purchasing power of the product in terms of the goods and services finally consumed and invested [5, p. 51]. Of these three sources of income, the last mentioned reflects the difference between the prices of the goods the nation produces (including exports) and the prices of the goods the nation consumes (the domestic production it keeps for its own consumption, plus the imports it gets for its exports) — that is, it includes gains or losses from change in the nation's foreign "terms of trade."[6]

Relative price changes in the present context mean, of course, changes in individual prices relative to the general price level. It follows that the gains or losses from the differential price changes that accrue to individual sectors of an economy must largely offset one another. For a country as a whole, then, the treatment of relative price changes will be of little moment.[7] This is hardly ground, however, for believing that it is equally unimportant for individual sectors of the economy, or for individual companies.

Let me make sure that what I am saying is not read to mean something I do not want to say. I am *not* saying that current replacement costs should be ignored, and attention focused only on original cost (adjusted or unadjusted for changes in the general price level), when businessmen or others make decisions on pricing, or production, or material purchases, or renewal of leases, or investment in additional plant and equipment. No economist taught the meaning of Jevons' "bygones are bygones" would say this. Current — and prospective — replacement prices *must* be taken into account in deciding what to do. But when calculating realized profits, the gains

as gains or losses "on capital account" — that is, to include them among the capital gains or losses restricted to the surplus account — or as items in the current income accounts; and (2) whether to show the effects in the accounts when they are recognized, even though not actually "realized," or only when they are realized. To inform all interested parties, it is necessary to show these effects when they are recognized, rather than wait until they are realized, even though this would require rough estimation; and to treat them as current income account items. However, I would propose putting this information, along with the information on the effects of changes in the general price level, in a supplement to the usual reports — in this case, also preferably a supplement that would cover an accounting period much longer than the usual 12-month period.

[6]I should add that the method of deflating exports and imports used by the Department of Commerce eliminates from national product and income these gains or losses from changes in the country's foreign terms of trade [10, pp. 446-7]. For a small country heavily engaged in foreign trade, this procedure could introduce a serious error into the estimates.

[7]Provided foreign trade and change in the foreign terms of trade are small. I am skirting, here, a controversial point — mentioned in the preceding footnote — in the theory of national accounts: I am assuming that national income is defined to include gains or losses from changes in the foreign terms of trade and that the general price level is defined as the IPI for national income so defined.

or losses from differential price movements may not be ignored.[8]   If a numerical example is necessary, then consider the case of merchandise purchased by a retailer for $1,000 in period one and sold in period two for $1,500.   In the ordinary accounting calculation, the profit (ignoring other costs) would be recorded as $500.   Suppose the general price level had risen between period one and period two by 10 percent, and the unit price of the merchandise had risen by 20 percent.   The calculation of material cost at replacement prices (current prices) would yield a profit of $300 ($1,500 − $1,200).   Properly calculated for general price-level changes only, profit in terms of the period two price level would be $400 ($1,500 − $1,100).   This $400 equals the $300 plus a profit of $100 owing to a relative price change. (In terms of period one price levels, the profit would be $364 = $1,364 − $1,000.   The $400 is 10 percent more than the $364 because the period two price level is 10 percent above the period one price level.)   Conversion to replacement cost prices excludes what should not be excluded: the effects of relative price changes.

This criticism is applicable, with some qualifications, to LIFO as it is ordinarily used in accounting for withdrawals from inventory. LIFO substitutes current-period prices for prior-period prices and thus adjusts for hetero-temporality, but it also "adjusts out" the profits or losses sustained on inventories when relative prices change. Inventories are priced at "first-in" prices, which may be much below current prices or even actual cost during a period of inflation.   Should the physical volume of inventories be reduced, however, profits reported under LIFO would not be free of price-level hetero-temporality. Indeed, in effect, all the previous adjustments would be canceled, and the full difference between book prices and current prices, which reflects the cumulative rise in the general price level (plus or minus change in relative prices) would be included in the calculated profits.

A similar, though less sharp, criticism may be made of the Inventory Valuation Adjustment, used by the Office of Business Economics of the Department of Commerce in its calculations of the national accounts [28].   This procedure is as follows: the difference between the change in the book value of inventories and the value of the change in the physical volume of inventories (valued at the current prices of the goods held in inventory) is the amount taken to be the Inventory Valuation Adjustment (IVA). This amount is subtracted from profits to reach an adjusted profits figure.   In this way the IVA removes the change in book values due

---

[8]Perhaps one of the objectives of those who advocate replacement cost accounting is "conservatism." To state profits conservatively, in this way, is almost by definition, also to state profits inaccurately.

I doubt that anyone would advocate eliminating the effects of relative price movements if the relevant absolute price movements were downward.

to change in relative prices as well as to change in the general price level. It is easy to see that if the physical volume of inventories were to remain unchanged, the IVA would equal the full change in the book value of inventories, including any change in relative prices. The IVA thus eliminates from profits an item of profit that should not be eliminated.[9]

Interpretation of the charging of depreciation at replacement costs is considerably more complicated. It still remains largely a subject for discussion rather than an accounting practice. Even in the national accounts, few countries follow this procedure. However, something needs to be said about it.[10]

If it is assumed, as it generally is, that the quantity of capital consumed can be determined by means of a fairly simple depreciation formula that is independent of price change —straight-line, or declining-balance, for example — then this is the quantity to be multiplied by the replacement cost of the capital goods to get the depreciation charge in current prices. In effect, capital assets would be treated as inventories are in the national accounts: the current value of net capital formation would be taken equal to the net change in physical assets multiplied by the current replacement cost of such assets.[11] The contribution of relative price changes to profits would be eliminated, and depreciation charges at replacement cost would be subject to the same criticism as the IVA or LIFO.

The analogy between inventories and capital assets is imperfect, however. One may also — and I would argue more correctly — consider the proper depreciation (and obsolescence) charge to be the actual (necessarily estimated) decline, or anticipated decline, in the current value of the relevant capital asset.[12] This decline would

---

[9]The procedure followed by the OBE is quite correct for estimating the National Product, as I have said elsewhere [10, pp. 444–6]. I am not questioning the IVA for that purpose.

[10]In the United States, the historical estimates of national income and product provided by the NBER make use of replacement cost accounting for depreciation [20]. This is not true, however, of the currently available official national accounts published by the Department of Commerce (except for depreciation on farm plant and equipment, the estimates for which are provided by the Department of Agriculture). Although the Department of Commerce has not yet put replacement-cost depreciation charges into its official accounts, it has made valuable estimates of these depreciation charges in its Capital Stock Study [16, 31 and 32]. These are utilized below.

[11]Gross capital formation, which is already at current prices, less capital consumption at current prices, equals net capital formation at current prices.

[12]Cp. Hotelling [18]. The relevant current value is the cost, delivered and installed, to a normal buyer, *not* what the owner of the asset would get for it if he disposed of it in the second hand market.

The usual question arises concerning the accounting treatment of differences between the decline in value that is anticipated and the decline in value that actually occurs. As I have already implied, I would go along with treating the differences as surplus account items in the annual statements, but would favor treating them as income account items in statements covering a longer fiscal period, say 5 or 10 years. Long fiscal period statements, it goes without saying, would have to be expressed in dollars of fixed general purchasing power if the figures were to make sense. I am puzzled by the lack of interest of accountants in such long-period accounts.

reflect changes in the replacement cost of the capital asset, if it were still being produced (which is not always the case), as well as wear and tear. It would also reflect obsolescence of the capital asset due to technological improvements in later vintages of the capital asset or in substitute capital goods, changes in maintenance and operating costs due to changes in relative prices of labor and materials, as well as wear and tear, changes in the demand for the product turned out with the help of the capital asset, and changes in interest rates. In short, the decline in current value would reflect (1) the current value of the depreciation and obsolescence that has occurred (or is estimated to have occurred) plus (2) the change in the value of the asset due to change in the general price level. The first item, the "correct" charge at current prices, would not exclude changes in relative prices. If the usual procedure, described in the preceding paragraph, were to be viewed as a rough approximation to the second procedure, depreciation at replacement cost would not be subject to the criticism that it excludes relative price changes. But this view could hardly be held of depreciation based on the straight-line depreciation formula.

THE PROBLEM OF FIXED DOLLAR PAYMENTS

When inflation is expected over the term of a loan, an escalator clause — or other arrangement that reserves equity rights — may be inserted in what would otherwise be a fixed-payment contract. Alternatively, adjustment to inflation may take the form of a higher interest rate — higher, of course, by the expected rate of increase in the general price level. This arrangement may pose an accounting problem, and a source of error in the use of the usual accounting reports, that is not met by the adjustments already proposed.

Consider the case of a firm that borrows on a long-term loan at a fixed interest rate, for example, in order to finance its operations during a period of inflation. Suppose, also, that the firm's selling prices and the prices it pays for materials, etc., move up with the general price level. The firm's costs of operation — including interest charges — relative to gross income would then tend to be higher in the earlier years and lower in the later years of the term covered by the loan than over the term as a whole. Correspondingly, the firm's net income, as ordinarily calculated, would be lower during the earlier years and higher during the later years than its average net income during the period of the loan. Deflation of the reported annual net income by an index of the general price level could only partially correct the reported income. Part of the reported costs in the earlier years, even after correction for changes in the price level, would in fact simply be an advance payment that should properly be charged to the operations of later years. In addition to a price-level adjustment, then, what would be required is an annual series of accounting entries to redistribute costs and profits over the term of the loan in such a way as to equalize the expected annual rates of return.

Obviously, the accounts of creditors as well as debtors would be affected. While the problem would appear most prominently in dealing with debt arrangements, essentially the same problem would be encountered in dealing with other fixed-dollar-payment arrangements, such as rentals, long-term price contracts, and wage and salary contracts. (In these, however, recourse to escalator clauses will be more frequent.) Convertible debentures, convertible preferred stocks, and lease-back arrangements raise additional accounting problems which can only be mentioned here.

The problem described in the present section will be of minimal importance to firms that borrow on a short term basis (relative to the length of their fiscal periods), or finance their operations through a more or less continuous series of long-term contracts. The problem will be much more important for firms that borrow heavily on a long-term basis at infrequent intervals. In a period of inflation, their reported profits will require the adjustment mentioned if these profits are to be comparable with the profits of earlier or later years, or with the profits of other companies.

CLUES TO THE MAGNITUDE OF THE ADJUSTMENTS

CHANGES IN INDEXES OF THE GENERAL PRICE LEVEL

The several steps required to adapt the accounts to changing general price levels are of different degrees of importance. One or two of the adjustments may, in fact, strike the reader as picayune, and not worth a second thought. This can certainly turn out to be the case. It seemed desirable, however, to state what adjustments were required in principle, and leave the question whether any or all of them were worthwhile, in any particular case, to this section of our discussion.

Whether an adjustment is important or not depends not only on what difference it would make in the figures, but also on the standards of precision at which the user of the figures aims — which depends, in turn, on his purpose. Let us concentrate here on the first point, the quantitative difference that the adjustments would make in reported profits and rates of return.

Clearly, the importance of any of the adjustments depends, first of all, on the rate of change in the general price level.[13]

I have already noted a few summary facts on the rate of increase in the general price level and expressed the opinion that the increase has been far from negligible in the United States in recent decades. The figures in Chart 1[14] give the full picture for 1913-68 as revealed by the three currently available indexes often used to measure changes in general price level. Certainly, as far as the period since 1913 is concerned, the contours traced by these three price indexes bear a distinct resemblance to one another. All three show the sharp price rise and then decline associated with World War I and its aftermath, the slight rise and decline during the rest of the 1920's, the decline during the Great Contraction, the swing up to 1937 and then decline to 1939, the rise during World War II and then in the late 1940's when price ceilings were lifted, the Korean flare-up, the slow rate of increase after the middle 1950's and the recent acceleration. Chart 2 gives the annual percentage changes in the IPI, together with changes over the somewhat longer periods defined by business-cycle phases. During the 40-year period beginning with 1929, the GNP IPI rose at an average rate of 2.3 percent per annum, the CPI at 1.8 percent, and the WPI at 1.9 percent. But though the main outlines of the three indexes are much the same, there are differences. Especially interesting between 1958 and 1964 is the negligible change in the WPI while the other two continued to march upward. And there are some differences, also, between the IPI and the CPI [14]. Which of the three indexes is best for measuring the general price level?

The CPI covers the consumption goods and services purchased only by urban wage earners and lower salaried workers [29]. Although this is a large fraction of what is consumed by the nation, it is not the whole of it and it fails to cover business investment goods and government expenditure. The IPI does cover the full range of goods and services on which the national income is spent, and is superior to the CPI on that account. It is, in fact, essentially a weighted average of the CPI (with upward adjustments in the weights of the consumption goods bought by the higher-income groups) and indexes of the prices of investment goods and of government purchases with the CPI given the preponderant weight that it deserves [28]. The WPI, although often referred to as a measure of inflation,

[13]This needs a small qualification: one of our adjustments is the "correction" of the accounts for the exclusion — by replacement cost accounting — of the effect on income of relative price changes. These relative price changes will be much more important than general price changes when the latter are small. However — this is why the qualification is minor — replacement cost accounting would hardly ever be used, or the question even discussed, were changes in the general price level small.

[14]Sources of figures in the charts are given in Appendix 2.

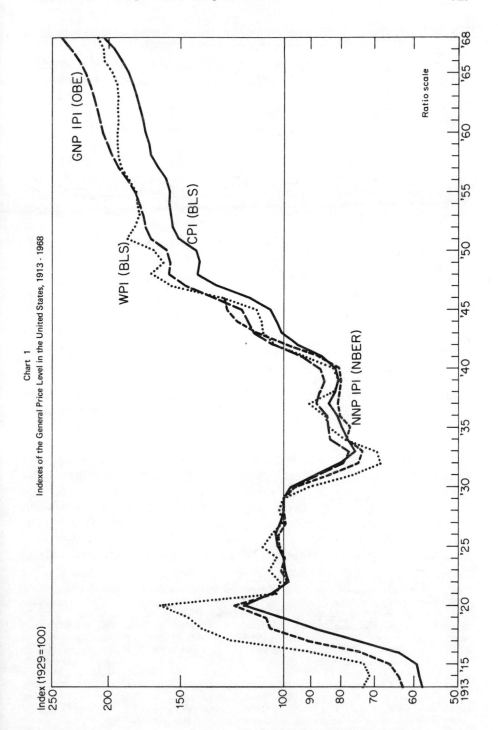

Chart 1

Indexes of the General Price Level in the United States, 1913 - 1968

Index (1929=100)

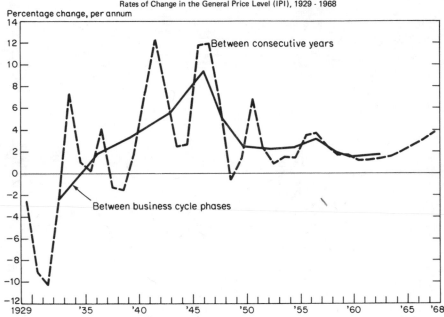

Chart 2
Rates of Change in the General Price Level (IPI), 1929 - 1968

especially by businessmen, is clearly inferior to either the IPI or the CPI for our purpose. The WPI omits services, construction, and other important categories of goods and services on which incomes are spent; prices the tangible goods it covers at the wholesale stage, which precedes the stage at which most final expenditures are made; and combines the prices of the goods covered with inappropriate weights [29].[15]

None of the indexes is perfect, by any means, and one indication of this is the difference between the two IPI's shown in the chart for 1929–46. One of these is the currently available Department of Commerce's implicit price deflator for GNP. The other is an historical

---

[15]In this connection see the report by the Price Statistics Review Committee of the NBER [23] (the "Stigler report"); also Gainsbrugh and Backman [14]. One thoughtful businessman expressed a preference for the WPI over the CPI and IPI in the following words: "Give me five years of stable wholesale prices, and I think I can assure you of a healthy non-inflationary economic environment and a reasonably good bond market in spite of the upcreep in both of the other two indices." This can be interpreted as saying that when the WPI is stable, inflation cannot be a very serious problem — which is surely correct, for there are limits on the degree of divergence between the WPI and the other two indexes. But it is not obvious that the WPI would or could long remain stable if there were a continuous upcreep in the CPI and the IPI. Nor is it correct to say that a stable WPI means no inflation. If the WPI remains stable when the other two are going up, this must be because productivity in the pre-retail stages of tangible commodity production is rising more rapidly than productivity in the economy at large. In the absence of inflation the WPI would decline in these circumstances, not remain stable.

series, not currently published, prepared at the NBER by Simon Kuznets [20] and extended through the World War II period by Milton Friedman and Anna Schwartz [13]. The Department of Commerce index differs from the NBER index partly because the latter related to NNP rather than GNP. More important, the NBER index includes a rough allowance for wartime black market prices, not made in the Department of Commerce index.

There are, in fact, a considerable number of questions about the IPI, as there are about the CPI and WPI, which are better reserved for another occasion.[16] Some of these deficiencies appear to be quite minor, and some may tend to offset one another. The resulting total error is probably not as serious as a longish list of deficiencies might suggest.

The fact that the price indexes are imperfect is not a good objection to their use, however. Nor has it prevented them from being put to practical use. Despite their many deficiencies, the CPI and WPI appear in the escalator provisions of thousands of wage and purchase contracts. And the IPI, with all its imperfections, directly or indirectly affects national judgments and discussions of a most momentous sort.[17]

---

[16]Briefly, questions arise about: (1) the appropriate concept of a general price level, particularly whether or for what purposes it should cover — as did Carl Snyder's famous index — transactions in property such as real estate and stocks and bonds, services of labor at all stages of production, etc., as well as the goods and services that enter GNP; (2) the choice among various concepts of GNP, which may differ from the Department of Commerce concept in the treatment of government (particularly with regard to the treatment of government property and government services to business), education, R & D, etc.; (3) the choice between a GNP and NNP IPI; (4) whether and how to allow for the increase in productivity in government, construction, and the service industries, which current calculations of GNP in the United States largely ignore; (5) whether and how to correct for improvements in the quality of these and other goods and services — improvements not taken into account by present methods of defining and measuring price changes; and (6) the accuracy of the basic price data — particularly, to what extent the list prices of sellers correctly reflect the prices actually paid by buyers. Research on these questions is proceeding at the NBER and elsewhere.

[17]When biases in the price statistics, particularly the failure to cover quality improvements adequately, are being discussed, it is important to remember, first, that not all quality improvements are over-looked. The methods used by the BLS (especially in computing the CPI) do pick up some of the quality improvements and adjust the price statistics accordingly. Second, as has already been pointed out, the quality bias that may exist in the CPI or IPI may be unimportant. Third, it may also be irrelevant for some purposes. For example, to low-income groups that are forced to uptrade — that is, to buy better qualities of medical services, or other goods or services, than they want or can afford — the higher price is truly a price rise [24]. Fourth, to the same degree that the IPI is biased upward, because of quality improvement, the real GNP index is biased downward. To correct the rate of increase of the general price level must entail a corresponding correction in the opposite direction, in real GNP — and therefore also in national output per manhour. Consider, for example, a money-wage guidepost which combines an improvement factor and an escalator clause, such as made the headlines in 1948 when the GM-UAW contract was signed. (Such a guidepost is more like the guidepost of the Cabinet Committee on Price Stability, reported at the turn of the year, than like the original 1962 guideposts of the Council of Economic Advisers.) If the escalator factor (which is based on the price index) is corrected downward, the improvement factor (which is based on the index of output per manhour) must be corrected upward, and by an equal proportion.

The crucial question is not whether changes in the general price level can be measured with great accuracy, but rather whether a dollar adjusted for change in its purchasing power even roughly is not a more useful monetary unit than an unadjusted dollar. When the price level is changing very slowly, the answer may well be in the negative, and indeed the question would not be asked when that is the case. When the price level is changing at a Brazilian rate, or even a Japanese rate, the answer must surely be in the affirmative. When it is rising at the rate shown in the chart, the answer is less clear. Opinions will differ. But as I have said, even two percent more per annum mounts up — in ten years, to a rise of 22 percent, in twenty years, to a rise of almost 50 percent. It is doubtful that correction for the improvements in quality that are now ignored, for example, and other desirable corrections of the price indexes, would shrink the increases to negligible amounts.

Accepting the IPI as a measure of change in the purchasing power of the dollar, it is easy enough to convert existing figures on profits — which are expressed in dollars of changing (and rather mixed — hetero-temporal) purchasing power — into figures expressed in dollars of reasonably constant purchasing power. The level of the adjusted profits will depend, of course, on the base chosen. If the adjusted profits were to be expressed in terms of 1958 prices, say, rather than 1929 prices, the line tracing the adjusted profits would be raised in the proportion that the 1958 price level bears to the level of 1929. But the percentage rates of change of the adjusted profits would be largely unaffected.[18] Whichever base were chosen, the slope of the trend of the adjusted figures would be considerably less steep than the slope of the trend of book profits.

This simple adjustment would, as I have said, take us a long way along the path to a fully adjusted income figure in most cases. But it does not take care of the problem of hetero-temporality, to which we now turn.

THE INVENTORY VALUATION ADJUSTMENT

The available estimates relate entirely to calculations of re-placement cost. We first consider the effects of replacement cost

---

[18]I say "largely" because the rate of change of a price index is influenced by its weight-base. If the IPI used to obtain 1958 purchasing-power figures were a Laspeyres or other index calculated on the 1958 base year, or on that plus the given year (as in the Edgeworth), it would differ from the corresponding index used to obtain the 1929 purchasing power figures and therefore calculated on the 1929 base year. However, calculations by the Department of Commerce and others generally reveal only small differences between differently based indexes over the period. since 1929. For alternative calculations covering the period 1965-68, see [33]. The Department of Commerce IPI is essentially a chain of several links, each of which is largely a Paasche index.

accounting for materials consumed, as indicated by the Department of Commerce estimates of its Inventory Valuation Adjustment.

As has already been mentioned, the IVA is designed to adjust not for changes in the general price level, but rather for the price changes that result from the turnover of inventory — that is, for changes in the prices of the goods handled on an inventory basis. Further, the intention of the IVA is not to express the consumption of goods taken out of inventory in terms of constant prices but rather in terms of current or replacement prices.   In short, the IVA shifts material consumption from historical cost prices to replacement cost prices — which means an adjustment for hetero-temporality of general price levels *plus* an adjustment for changes in relative prices.

The behavior of the IVA (Chart 3) indicates, as might be expected — the kinds of goods treated on an inventory basis being

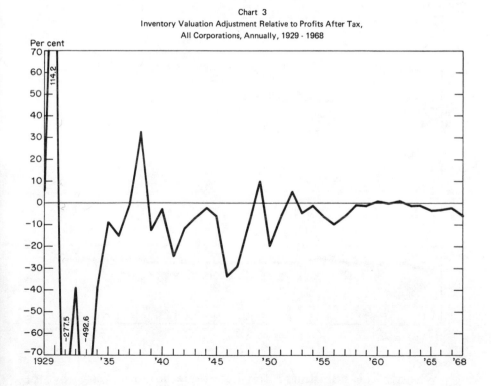

Chart 3
Inventory Valuation Adjustment Relative to Profits After Tax,
All Corporations, Annually, 1929 - 1968

what they are — that cyclical changes in these relative prices are rather prominent. Were the IVA limited to adjusting inventories for the hetero-temporality of the general price level, the series would be smoother, and there would be fewer than the nine positive adjustments shown. Nevertheless, the other 30 of the 39 annual adjustments for 1929–68 are negative. On the average, then, reported profits are shown to be too high.

A more explicit estimate (by the OBE) of the lag of book values of goods in inventory behind their replacement costs for a shorter period is given in Chart 4. During 1947–68, when the price trend was upward, the lag resulted in replacement costs being generally higher than original costs.

Chart 4

Indexes of Prices Underlying Book Values and Replacement
Costs Per Unit, Nonfarm Business Inventories,
1947 - 1968 (1958 Prices = 100)

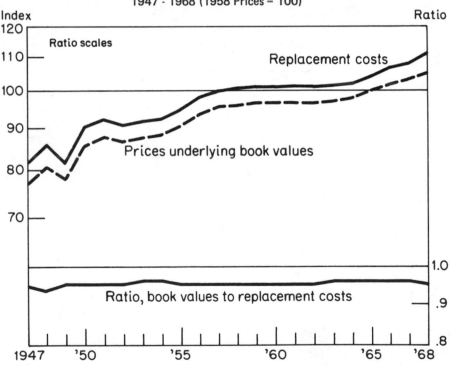

Whether the adjustment for hetero-temporality made by the IVA's lowers the level of reported profits more or less than would a general price level adjustment alone depends on the behavior of the ratio of the prices of the goods handled on an inventory basis to the prices of goods in general. When this ratio falls, as was the case during 1947–68, according to OBE estimates of the replacement costs of goods drawn from inventories (Chart 5), there is a loss from differential price movements.[19] The IVA then makes for a lesser downward adjustment of profits than would the general price level adjustment we want.

Chart 5

Indexes of the General Price Level (IPI) and of Replacement Costs
Per Unit for Inventory Withdrawals and for Depreciation Charges,
1947 - 1968

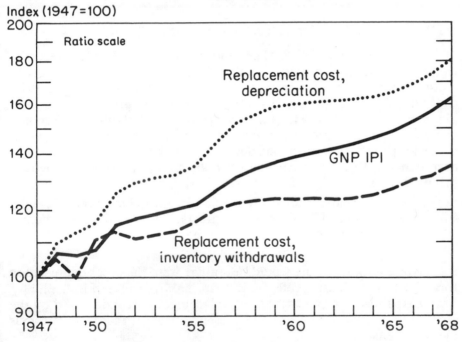

The IVA adjustment for the period 1929-68 as a whole[20] averages to − 2.8 percent of profits before tax, and about double that for profits after tax. For the period beginning with 1953, the ratio is less, but still of some significance. This suggests that an adjustment for hetero-temporality of the price level may be worth looking into further.

---

[19]The decline in the ratio is not surprising. The average price of movable goods (which is essentially what the WPI measures) fell between 1947 and 1968 in relation to the IPI (which measures changes in the prices of services and construction, as well as movable goods). (See Chart 1.)

[20]This ratio is a weighted average calculated by first deflating each year's profits and each year's IVA, and then taking the ratio of the sums.

The importance of the IVA, relative to profits, varies considerably among industries. There are two reasons — variation in the relative importance of materials in total cost, and variation also in the relative volatility of the prices of the materials used by each industry. We cannot be sure, therefore, that the industrial variation in the IVA adjustment tells us what we want to know. But, as before, it is at least suggestive — perhaps more than merely suggestive, for, as might be expected, the IVA is most important for wholesale and retail trade (averaging 7 or 8 percent of profits after tax, during 1953–67). It is least important for the public utilities (averaging about 1 percent of profits after tax, during 1953–67).

DEPRECIATION AT REPLACEMENT COST

Studies by the NBER [7], Goldsmith [15], and more recently, by the OBE [31,32] provide us with information on historical cost, constant-price cost, replacement cost depreciation, and related price changes. Chart 6 gives one set of the relevant price indexes — replacement (current) costs and the prices underlying depreciation charges — and the ratio of the one index to the other. These were calculated on the assumption that depreciation charges are distributed in accordance with the straight-line formula, using the Treasury Department's Bulletin "F" depreciation rates [30].

Over the years, the straight-line formula has been partially superseded by several "accelerated depreciation" formulas, and depreciation rates above Bulletin "F" levels have been permitted [31 and 32, 27].

However, the picture would be similar were the other depreciation formulas followed, using rates up to a third above those in Bulletin "F." This is true also for an alternative replacement cost index used by the OBE in its calculations. For the present purpose, then, Chart 6 tells the story reasonably well.

Because pre-World War I levels were still heavily imbedded in the books of account even as late as 1929, the prices underlying depreciation charges in the year were still below replacement costs. This was the case, in fact, in all the years covered except for the lowest two of the Great Depression years. The gap was greatest, roundly 35 percent of the replacement cost, in 1948. The difference between depreciation prices and replacement prices then gradually diminished until it reached about 15 percent in 1968. (Under the double-declining, shorter life formula, the difference was about 25 percent of replacement cost in 1948 and 10 percent in 1968.) During the whole of the post World War II period, changes in the general price level (which took

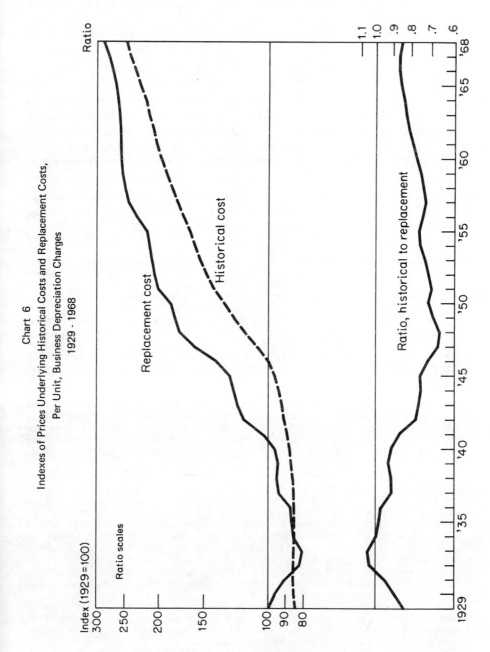

Chart 6
Indexes of Prices Underlying Historical Costs and Replacement Costs,
Per Unit, Business Depreciation Charges
1929 - 1968

place before, as well as during the period) caused profits in current prices to be overstated — by an amount equal, of course, to the difference mentioned.[21]

Just as with the IVA, a shift from historical to replacement cost would exclude (unfortunately, for our purpose) the contribution to profits of changes in relative prices. In this case, the cost of replacing capital plant and equipment rose in relation to the general price level over most of the period (Chart 5).[22] This means that holders of plant and equipment gained something from the differential price movement — a gain that is excluded from adjusted profits by replacement cost accounting. A shift to replacement costs would thus bring the level of profits down somewhat more than we would want for our purpose.

As in the case of the IVA, industries differ with regard to the correction required for the hetero-temporality of depreciation charges.

---

[21]Whether the liberalization of depreciation practices that took place after 1940, mentioned above, has provided an offset to the over-statement of profits caused by a rising general price level is discussed below in the final section entitled, "Errors in the Use of Unadjusted Accounting Reports."

It has sometimes been argued that an offset is provided also by the technological changes that improve the quality or productivity of plant and equipment — changes that also complicate the problem of measuring changes in the general price level, as already noted.

The point can be put as follows: When inflation occurs, depreciation charges calculated at original cost become insufficient to finance the replacement of capital assets at the expiration of their service lives. (Calculations useful in this connection have been provided by Evsey Domar [6].) Capital cannot be maintained, except by using funds taken out of profits as these are ordinarily computed. This is why we say that profits are overstated when inflation occurs. However, if technological change causes the capacity to produce, per unit of plant and equipment, also to rise — at a rate that is equal to the rate of increase in the price level — depreciation calculated at original cost will be sufficient to finance the maintenance of capacity.

But the depreciation charge on a capital asset is not designed to measure the decline in its capacity. The purpose is to measure the decline in the value of the asset. This value is a function not only of capacity, but also of the number of years of remaining life and of the other factors listed in an earlier footnote. Under certain assumptions — of which the "one-hoss-shay" assumption is only one — the capacity of a machine to produce may remain constant until the day the machine collapses into junk. But its value will nevertheless have been falling with the passage of time.

For some purposes, of course, it is capacity to produce rather than value of assets that is relevant. (That is why the capital-output ratio, which has more to do with value than with capacity, is an inadequate criterion in development planning.) But this purpose is not our purpose. (Is it necessary to add that if the rate of inflation should exceed the rate of improvement in the quality of capital goods, depreciation changes would be insufficient to maintain even capacity?)

Closely related is the suggestion that growth in the volume of capital assets provides an offset to inflation. Growth keeps low the fraction of depreciation charges (or of expenditures on capital assets) required for replacement. Depreciation charges are then in excess of the amount required to maintain capacity. But the presumption that this provides an offset to the understatement of depreciation caused by inflation, is correct only if the objective is to measure changes in capacity, not changes in value.

[22]Mention was made above of an alternate replacement cost series — "Price Series 2." Price Series 2 has risen less rapidly than Price Series 1, but the difference is not great. However, it is not negligible and further corrections that have been proposed would enlarge the difference. (Substitution of the plant and equipment replacement cost series used by the OBE in its national accounts by a series that rose less rapidly would affect also the IPI; but the proportionate adjustment would be very much smaller.)

This, as is well-known, is because the average length of life of capital assets and the relative importance of capital assets vary among industries.

PROFITS IN CONSTANT PRICES

We put the preceding estimates together, blinking our eyes to the problem of relative price changes, in Chart 7. The result gives us at least a notion of what corporate profits would look like — were depreciation charges calculated consistently on a straight-line basis, at Bulletin "F" rates — if adjusted for changes in the general price level.

Chart 7
Profits After Tax, Nonfinancial Corporations,
Before and After Adjustments for Changes in the General Price Level
1929 - 1968

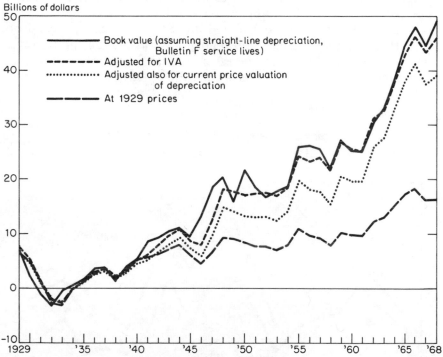

The series in the chart relate to all nonfinancial corporations combined. They are, then, weighted averages of the series for individual companies. All companies have experienced essentially the same changes in the general price level, but the impact on their profits has not been the same. The profits of some companies must have been less affected, and those of other companies more affected, than the average pictured in the chart. Comparisons among companies of levels of profits and of changes in profits are in some degree defective.

CORRECTED RATES OF RETURN

Economists making comparisons of the profit rates of different companies or industries have thought price level changes to be sufficiently important to warrant drawing attention to the probable effects on the comparisons. Recently, George Stigler made an effort to correct for these effects [25]. The corrections are necessarily rather crude, for even had the required details been available, which was not the case, it would have been too burdensome a job to use the details to make special corrections for each of the many industries being compared. However, even these estimates provide some sense of the difference made by price adjustments. (See Chart 8.)

The rates of return calculated by Stigler refer to net profits after taxes as a percentage of total corporate assets (excluding investments in other companies). The estimates are for twenty-three groups of manufacturing industries. As is desirable, Stigler corrects separately

Chart 8

Rates of Return on Assets, at Book Value and at 1947 Prices,
Manufacturing Corporations, 1938 - 1958

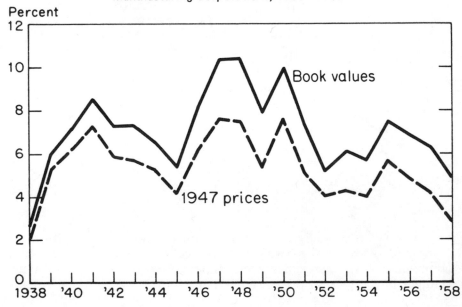

both numerator and denominator of the profit ratio. The price data used are essentially the same as those in the OBE's capital stock study and the corrections are therefore in terms of replacement cost rather than in terms of the general price level.

We may note, first, that the rates of return in 1947 prices are lower than the rates of return according to "book" in every year covered in Chart 8. In 1947 the corrected rate for manufacturing as a whole was 7.6 percent, for example, as compared with the book rate of return of 10.4 percent. In 1957 the two rates were 4.1 and 6.3 percent, respectively. Second, the difference between the two rates varied considerably among the 23 industries included in the analysis. The median difference in 1947 was 2.4, with an interquartile range of 1.1. In 1957 the variation was less, but so was the median profit rate. Chart 9 gives the full information.

It should be remembered that the industry figures hide whatever intra-industry variation there may be. Undoubtedly such variation exists, and the occasional calculations that have been made suggest that it is considerable.

ERRORS IN THE USE OF UNADJUSTED ACCOUNTING REPORTS

LIBERALIZED DEPRECIATION PRACTICES: AN OFFSET?

The question with which we are concerned is the bias in conventional accounting reports caused by the neglect of changes in the general price level. And we are concerned with the question because errors can result when these biased reports are put to the uses they are intended to serve. These errors would be of little consequence, however, were the reports subjected to other adjustments — adjustments that, although not aimed directly at the price-level problem, had the effect of meeting it.

Reference has already been made to what some observers view as a source of such an offset. This is the liberalization of depreciation practices permitted by the Treasury Department after 1940.

The liberalization of depreciation practices, as accountants well know, took two main routes. One involved granting permission to taxpayers to use depreciation methods — the double-declining balance method and the sum-of-the-years'-digits method — to recover more of an asset's cost in the early years of its life than would be possible with the straight-line method. These accelerated depreciation methods became applicable under the Internal Revenue Code of 1954. The

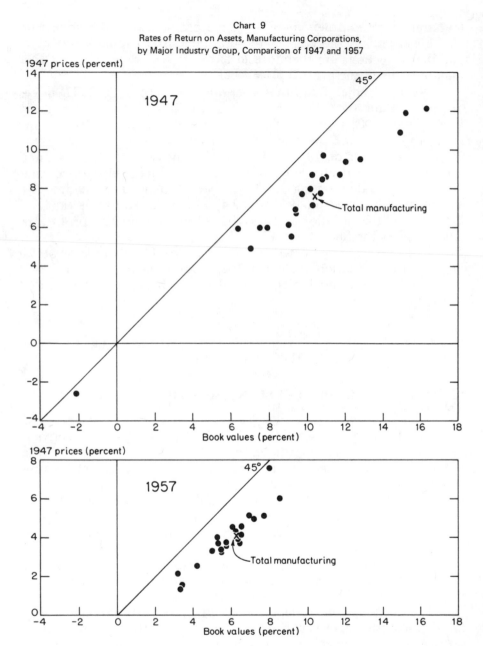

Chart 9
Rates of Return on Assets, Manufacturing Corporations,
by Major Industry Group, Comparison of 1947 and 1957

other kind of liberalization, which began with a Treasury Decision in 1934, allowed taxpayers to use shorter service lives than had

formerly been permissible.[23]   The details of the various changes
in the rules and regulations, and estimates of their effect on depreciation
charges (to which I shall refer in a moment), are set forth in Allen H.
Young's valuable articles [31, 32].

It can be shown, to begin with, that liberalization of depreciation
practices can take care of the problem created by a changing general
price level (if that is its objective) only temporarily. A shortening of
service life or a shift to a "faster" depreciation formula will obviously
raise depreciation charges above what they would have been under
the prior practice. And this increase in depreciation charges could
reduce reported profits to the level that would have been reached
were appropriate adjustments made for inflation. It could even push
profits below that level. But were inflation to continue, the offsetting
effects even of further reductions in service life and of shifts to still
faster depreciation formulas must eventually vanish.   At the limit,
when existing capital assets had been fully depreciated and newly
purchased capital assets were all being charged off immediately and
fully to current operations, even these current write-offs would not
be sufficient to keep profits at an appropriately deflated level.   A
rising (real) capital-output ratio could postpone this result, but there
are obvious limits to the continuation of such an upward trend.

Perhaps more important, in practice, is the strong likelihood that
steps in a policy of continual depreciation liberalization would not —
and could not — be geared to the rate of inflation and still less to
changes in this rate. Only by chance, therefore, could liberalization
provide a reasonably appropriate offset to the current rate of inflation
in any particular fiscal period. Also, as a general rule, the effectiveness
of depreciation liberalization in redressing the bias caused by inflation
would vary among industries, making industrial comparisons of rates
of return most difficult.

But we need not confine ourselves to these general remarks.
Young's calculations of depreciation charges for nonfinancial corporations under varying assumptions make it possible to be specific about
the quantitative effects of liberalization [32]. We focus our attention
on the depreciation calculated under two main assumptions, and to the
years as shown in Table 1.

Consider the depreciation charged in 1958, 21.3 billion dollars.
This closely approximated the depreciation that would have been
charged at historical cost valuation on a straight-line basis, using
Bulletin "F" service lives; plus another 5 billion estimated by Young
to show more liberalized depreciation practices.[24] Were depreciation

_____

[23]The investment tax credit, first enacted in the Revenue Act of 1962, is also relevant, but
I shall not try to deal with its effects.

[24]The 21.3 billion includes oil and gas well drilling and exploration costs charged to
current expense, plus certain other minor items specified by Young [32, Table 1].

TABLE 1

	1929	1948	1958	1966
	(unit: billion dollars)			
Straight-line depreciation, Bulletin "F" service lives				
Historical cost valuation	4.4	6.4	16.7	29.8
Current price valuation	5.4	9.9	23.0	35.0
Double-declining balance depreciation, .75 Bulletin "F" service lives				
Historical cost valuation	5.4	8.5	21.6	37.8
Current price valuation	5.9	11.2	26.0	41.2
Depreciation actually charged	4.1	6.8	21.3	37.0

estimated on a straight-line, "F" service lives basis, at *current* price valuation, considered to be the more appropriate charge, the amount would have been 23.0 billion. It is clear, in this case and for this year, that liberalization came fairly close towards permitting, in effect, depreciation to be charged on a current-price basis. In 1966, depreciation under the liberalized regulations actually exceeded the current-price amount estimated on the basis of straight-line, "F" service lives. (In 1929 and 1948, liberalization played little or no role.) But in neither 1958 nor 1966 did liberalization serve to convert current-price depreciation charges or calculated profits to a constant purchasing-power basis. As Chart 7 indicates, this is the most important step in meeting the problem of inflation.

Shifting our attention, suppose the double-declining balance method, with 75 percent of Bulletin "F" lives, were considered to be the appropriate way to determine depreciation charges at historical cost. In that case, actual charges (including liberalization) in 1958 would have provided no offset whatever to the error resulting from determining the charges at historical rather than current prices. And, as in the case of the straight-line, Bulletin "F" practice, no allowance would have been made for changes in the general price level.

We have been assuming what some people seem to suggest, that the sole objective of the liberalization of depreciation practices was to deal with the problem of inflation. If this was indeed the objective, it is evident that liberalization is an inefficient and erratic way to reach it. In fact, however, it is questionable whether the assumption is entirely or even partly warranted. Some proponents of liberalized depreciation may indeed have had in mind its offset to the effects of inflation. It is also possible, however, that liberalization was designed to permit the abandonment of an unrealistic depreciation formula and table of permitted service lives already obsolete even in the 1920's. Or, alternatively, the purpose may have been to recognize that formulas and depreciation rates realistic enough before the war required revision in an era in which technological change, and the obsolescence to which it leads, was proceeding at an accelerated pace. To turn in still another direction, the objective could have been to provide a tax advantage to private capital formation simply in order to help sop up unemployment and raise the rate of economic growth. If so, we can say that inflation tended to nullify the steps taken in pursuit of this policy.

Whatever its objective, we may conclude that liberalization of depreciation has provided only a partial, if any, offset to the failure to adjust accounting records for inflation. Further, what offset it provided must have varied from one year to another, and from one industry or firm to another.

THE INEVITABILITY OF ERROR

Given that certain measurements are biased, it does not necessarily follow, as a matter of logic, that users of the measurements are seriously misled by them. All users might be aware, some even well aware, of what is going on. They might be able to make the adjustments themselves with "sufficient" accuracy, and indeed be in the habit of doing so more or less automatically. It is hardly conceivable, in any case, that all users of the unadjusted accounts would take them at their face value. On the other hand, it is equally doubtful that all users of the unadjusted accounts could entirely avoid being misled by them. Some degree of error is inevitable.

That the error must be limited hardly needs to be argued. It is not possible to take seriously a model of the economy in which money illusion is universal and persistent despite significant and continuing changes in the general price level. Although accountants may fail to adjust their reports for inflation, their reports are not the only source of information on what is happening. Nor is everybody unable to pay for and use this additional information. Nor, to pursue the question further, is it reasonable to suppose that users of this information would fail — in the very act of using it — to convey to others the implications of what is happening. In one way or another, and sooner or later, people learn from experience. I started out by saying that labor unions enter wage negotiations carrying briefcases crammed with consumer price indexes (as well as unadjusted profits figures!).

That error will not be entirely eliminated, however, is almost as obvious. Try to imagine an economy in which failure to adjust the accounts for inflation would have *no* significant effect on the decisions of users. Such an economy would need to have something like the following characteristics:[25] (1) Changes in prices, and therefore also in the general price level, would be open, not suppressed. No governmental regulations or private arrangements to control prices or foreign exchange rates or otherwise hide the effects of inflation, would be in force. (2) The general price level would be changing at a constant rate, and would have been doing so for a long time. There would be no "stop and go" in the policies and the other factors (including "exogenous" factors) that determine the general price level. (3) The denizens of this economy would all have finally learned what was happening, would know the past and current rate of inflation, could and would anticipate with confidence what the rate would be in the future, and would be accustomed to taking this "fact of life" into account in all their calculations and decisions. If some people lacked the capacity to acquire the knowledge and develop the habits appropriate to living and working in an inflationary economy, there would be enough competition to make those fully acquainted with the facts bring even the most ignorant up to par with the knowledgeable. Arrangements such as escalator clauses to cope with inflation could have become universal.[26]

These make up an obviously extreme set of assumptions. But they are even more extreme than they appear at first sight. Consider, for example, a fact to which we have already pointed — that every economy experiences technological change. For an economy to have the characteristics that have been specified, technological change would have to be absent. But technological change does take place, and as it does, shifts occur in the composition and durability of the equipment held by each company, and also, therefore, in the degree of hetero-temporality in every company's accounts. It would not be quite accurate, then, for the user of a company's accounts to lower the level of the company's reported profits (in order to express them in fully current dollars) by using the same proportional correction that he had been using in the past — even though the rate of inflation has not changed in the slightest. He would have to keep up with changing facts. He could not act in a routine manner.

Further, it is a fact that in few economies has inflation ever been entirely open, so that people could fully appreciate what had been happening. Rents, for example, tend to become fixed by laws setting ceilings, and foreign exchange rates to be controlled by quotas, special taxes, or other means. Sometimes, even, the published consumer price

[25]See Milton Friedman's Bombay Lectures [12].
[26]Compare Amotz Morag's "inflation-proof economy" [22].

indexes become biased through the "judicious" selection of the commodities being priced, or simply through failure to correct the sample of prices for obsolescence.

Nor, to turn to another of the assumptions, has inflation ever proceeded at a constant pace in any economy. Monetary and fiscal authorities are never able to offset accurately and quickly the effects of changes in exogenous factors. And no government has been able to stay in power without doing something — sooner or later, big or little, sensible or otherwise — about the inflation that is taxing so many, and thus causing the rate of inflation to change.

We could extend this list of the characteristics of an imaginary economy in which errors in the use of unadjusted accounting reports are largely absent. But I have said enough to make it clear that such an economy would not possess the characteristics of the economy with which we have to deal. It would be as unbelievable as an economy with persistent money illusion.

I have pointed to these models of imaginary economies in order to highlight some of the characteristics of the real world that must make for error, yet limit the degree of error, when accounting reports are unadjusted. Of course, the major source of error is inability to forecast. No improvement in the historical or current data could make forecasts errorless. But forecasts are surely better when founded on adequate records of the past and present. We do need to be concerned about the possibility of errors resulting from the use of unadjusted accounting reports.

The question, indeed, is not whether errors are entirely absent, or whether there is nothing but an irrational or ignorant faith in the unadjusted dollar or in the accounting reports that are made public. The question is, how much error is there? No clear answer is yet possible.

One could ask people what they know about inflation and how they take it into account in making their decisions. I suppose surveys of this kind have been made and that they provide some kernels of useful information. But I suspect, also, that the results are often ambiguous and difficult to interpret, as is attested by the experience of economists with surveys over many years.

Much better — at least potentially — would be an analysis of economic behavior in which one of the independent variables was the rate of change in the general price level. Whatever people may believe or say about themselves and their actions, what we want to know is how they actually behave when the general price level is steady or rising, or is rising slowly or rapidly, or is changing at a rate that varies from year to year. How different is the fraction of income saved, or a decision to invest or to hold cash, for example, in these different circumstances? Only in a few studies have fairly clear-cut results been obtained.[27] Recent work has been largely experimental, as is natural when the statistical data are still seriously limited in scope and often defective, and the emphasis has been mostly on technical econometric problems.

CONCLUDING COMMENTS

We are left, at this juncture, largely with opinions on the extent of the error resulting from the use of unadjusted accounting reports. But these opinions are not entirely arbitrary. To state explicitly what has already been implied, it is difficult to believe that many people can make their own adjustments to the accounts; or that when they try, that the results come at all close to being as accurate as they would be if accountants did the work; or that the social cost of making the adjustments would not be greatly reduced if the work were done by accountants for the use of all readers of company reports. In a word, it is reasonable to expect that business decisions would be sounder if the accounts were adjusted before reports were released.

The need for recognition of inflation extends beyond the sphere of corporation reports. The accounts of the federal, state, and local governments would also be substantially more useful, and subject to far less misunderstanding, if supplementary tabulations were appended to them setting forth the effects of price level changes. These tabulations need not be elaborate.

Adjustment of accounting reports for changes in the general price level would mean an improvement in only a small portion of the almost endless information needed for sound decisions. These decisions are of great importance, however. Improvement in any part of the information would be worth more than its cost.

---

[27]Mention may be made of Cagan's study of the demand for cash balances during periods of hyper-inflation [4], and of Friedman and Schwartz's study (among other things) of the lag between the changes that have occurred in the trend of the general price level and the effects of these changes on price expectations and interest rates [13].

BIBLIOGRAPHY

[1] American Institute of Certified Public Accountants. "Reporting the Financial Effects of Price-Level Changes." *Accounting Research Study No. 6.* New York: American Institute of Certified Public Accountants, Inc., 1963.

[2] Braithwaite, Stanley N. "Real Income Levels in Latin America." *The Review of Income and Wealth,* Series 14, No. 2 (June, 1968), pp. 113–82.

[3] Burns, Arthur F., and Wesley C. Mitchell. *Measuring Business Cycles.* New York: National Bureau of Economic Research, 1946.

[4] Cagan, Phillip. "The Monetary Dynamics of Hyperinflation." *Studies in the Quantity Theory of Money,* edited by Milton Friedman. Chicago: University of Chicago Press, 1956.

[5] Deane, Phyllis (editor). *Studies in Social and Financial Accounting.* International Association for Research in Income and Wealth. Income and Wealth Series IX. London: Bowes and Bowes, 1961.

[6] Domar, Evsey D. "Depreciation, Replacement, and Growth." *The Economic Journal,* Vol. LXIII (March, 1953), pp. 1–32; reprinted in Evsey D. Domar, *Essays in the Theory of Economic Growth.* New York: Oxford University Press, 1957.

[7] Fabricant, Solomon. *Capital Consumption and Adjustment.* New York: National Bureau of Economic Research, 1938.

[8] —————— . "Business Costs and Business Income Under Changing Price Levels." *New Responsibilities of the Accounting Profession.* New York: American Institute of Accountants, 1948; reprinted in Study Group on Business Income. *Five Monographs on Business Income.* New York: American Institute of Accountants, 1950.

[9] —————— . "The Varied Impact of Inflation on the Calculation of Business Income." *Current Business Studies.* New York: Institute of Trade and Commerce Professions, 1949; reprinted in Study Group on Business Income. *Five Monographs on Business Income.* New York: American Institute of Accountants, 1950.

[10] —————— . "Capital Consumption and Net Capital Formation," in Conference on Research in Income and Wealth. *A Critique of the United States Income and Product Accounts. Studies in Income and Wealth,* Vol. 22. Princeton: Princeton University Press, 1958.

[11] —————— . *A Primer on Productivity.* New York: Random House, 1969.

[12] Friedman, Milton. *Dollars and Deficits; Living with America's Economic Problems.* Englewood Cliffs, N. J.: Prentice-Hall, Inc., 1968.

[13] —————— , and Anna J. Schwartz. *Monetary Trends in the United States and the United Kingdom: Their Relation to Income, Prices, and Interest Rates.* National Bureau of Economic Research (in preparation).

[14] Gainsbrugh, Martin R., and Jules Backman. *Inflation and the Price Indexes.* Studies in Business Economics No. 94. New York: National Industrial Conference Board, Inc., 1966.

[15] Goldsmith, Raymond William. *A Study of Saving in the United States.* Princeton: Princeton University Press, 1955.

[16] Grose, Lawrence, Irving Rottenberg, and Robert C. Wasson. "New Estimates of Fixed Business Capital in the United States, 1925–65." *Survey of Current Business,* Vol. XLVI, No. 12 (December, 1966), pp. 34–40.

[17] Hastay, Millard. "The Cyclical Behavior of Investment," in a report of the National Bureau of Economic Research, Special Conference Series No. 4. *Regularization of Business Investment.* Princeton: Princeton University Press, 1954.

[18] Hotelling, Harold. "A General Mathematical Theory of Depreciation." *Journal of the American Statistical Association,* Vol. XX, No. 150 (September, 1925), pp. 340–53.

[19] Keynes, John Maynard. *A Treatise on Money.* London: Macmillan Co., 1930.

[20] Kuznets, Simon S. *Capital in the American Economy; Its Formation and Financing.* A Study by the National Bureau of Economic Research. Princeton: Princeton University Press, 1961.

[21] Moonitz, Maurice. "The Basic Postulates of Accounting." *Accounting Research Study No. 1.* New York: American Institute of Certified Public Accountants, 1961.

[22] Morag, Amotz. "For an Inflation-Proof Economy." *American Economic Review,* Vol. LII, No. 1 (March, 1962), pp. 177-85; reprinted in Amotz Morag. *On Taxes and Inflation.* New York: Random House, 1965.

[23] Price Statistics Review Committee of the National Bureau of Economic Research. *The Price Statistics of the Federal Government.* General Series No. 73. New York: National Bureau of Economic Research, Inc., 1961.

[24] Scitovsky, Anne A. "Changes in the Costs of Treatment of Selected Illnesses, 1951–65." *The American Economic Review,* Vol. LVII, No. 5 (December, 1967), pp. 1182–1195.

[25] Stigler, George J. *Capital and Rates of Return in Manufacturing Industries.* A Study by the National Bureau of Economic Research. Princeton: Princeton University Press, 1963.

[26] Study Group on Business Income. *Changing Concepts of Business Income.* Report of the Study Group on Business Income, American Institute of Accountants. New York: The Macmillan Company, 1952.

[27] Ture, Norman B. *Accelerated Depreciation in the United States, 1954-60.* National Bureau of Economic Research, Fiscal Study No. 9. New York: National Bureau of Economic Research, 1967.

[28] U.S. Department of Commerce, Office of Business Economics. *The National Income and Product Accounts of the United States, 1929-65; Statistical Tables,* a supplement to the *Survey of Current Business.* Washington: 1966.

[29] U. S. Department of Labor, Bureau of Labor Statistics. *Handbook of Labor Statistics 1967,* Bulletin No. 1555. Washington: 1967.

[30] U. S. Treasury Department, Bureau of Internal Revenue. *Bulletin "F,"
Income Tax Depreciation and Obsolescence; Estimated Useful
Lives and Depreciation Rates* (Revised January, 1942). Washington:
1942; reprinted as *Tables of Useful Lives of Depreciable Property.*
Washington: 1955.
[31] Young, Allan H. "Alternative Estimates of Corporate Depreciation
and Profits: Part I." *Survey of Current Business.* Vol. XLVIII,
No. 4 (April, 1968), pp. 17–28.
[32] —————— . "Alternative Estimates of Corporate Depreciation and
Profits: Part II." *Survey of Current Business.* Vol. XLVIII, No. 5
(May, 1968), pp. 16–28.
[33] —————— , and Claudia Harkins. "Alternative Measures of Price
Changes for GNP." *Survey of Current Business.* Vol. XLIX, No. 3
(March, 1969), pp. 47–52.

APPENDIX 1. CHARTS

1. Indexes of the General Price Level in the United States, 1913–1968.
2. Rates of Change in the General Price Level (IPI), 1929–1968.
3. Inventory Valuation Adjustment Relative to Profits after Tax, Corporations,
   Annually, 1929–1968.
4. Indexes of Prices Underlying Book Values and Replacement Costs per Unit,
   Nonfarm Business Inventories, 1947–1968.
5. Indexes of the General Price Level (IPI) and of Replacement Costs per Unit
   for Inventory Withdrawals and for Depreciation Charges, 1947–1968.
6. Indexes of Prices Underlying Historical Costs and Replacement Costs,
   per Unit, Business Depreciation Charges, 1919–1968.
7. Profits after Tax, Nonfinancial Corporations, before and after Adjustment
   for Changes in the General Price Level, 1929–1968.
8. Rates of Return on Assets, at Book Value and at 1947 Prices, Manufacturing
   Corporations, 1938–1958.
9. Rates of Return on Assets, Manufacturing Corporations, by Major Industry
   Group, Comparison of 1947 and 1957.

APPENDIX 2. SOURCES OF CHART DATA

1. The NNP IPI (Net National Product Implicit Price Index) is an unpublished series calculated at the National Bureau of Economic Research by Simon Kuznets [20], appendixes A and C for 1913-1942, and extended through 1946 by Milton Friedman and Anna Schwartz. The GNP IPI (Gross National Production Implicit Price Index) is from the Department of Commerce [28] and more recent issues of *Survey of Current Business*. The CPI and WPI are from the Bureau of Labor Statistics [29] and previous issues, and recent issues of *Monthly Labor Review*.

2. The rates of change in the General Price Level are computed from the OBE IPI mentioned above. The business cycle phases are as defined by the NBER [3] and unpublished data.

3. The IVA and the Corporate Profits after Tax (and before IVA) are from [28] and more recent issues of *Survey of Current Business*.

4. The implicit deflators are unpublished estimates prepared by the OBE, Department of Commerce.

5. See sources for Charts 1, 4 and 6.

6. The Historical Cost and the Replacement Cost indexes are from the OBE, Department of Commerce, Capital Stock Study; see Grose, Rottenberg, and Wasson [16]. The data are estimated on the basis of straight-line depreciation, using Bulletin "F" service lives, and the first of the two current price indexes prepared by the OBE.

7. The IVA is from [28] and more recent issues of *Survey of Current Business*. The Profits, Adjusted for IVA, the Depreciation Value Adjustment, and the Profits, Adjusted also for current price valuation of depreciation, are from Young [31 and 32] for 1929-1966; and estimates have been made for 1967 and 1968, based on Grose, Rottenberg, and Wasson [16]. The depreciation value adjustment is depreciation at current (replacement) cost less depreciation at historical cost. The data are estimated on the basis of straight-line depreciation, using Bulletin "F" service lives, and the first of the two current price indexes prepared by the OBE.

   The Profits, at 1929 prices, are the Profits after the above adjustments, deflated by the GNP IPI.

   The Profits, Book Value, are the Profits, Adjusted for IVA, less the Inventory Valuation Adjustment.

8. The Rates of Return are from Stigler [25], Table B-1, p. 203 and Errata, Table 5, p. 8. They are adjusted net profits after taxes divided by total corporate assets excluding investments in other companies. There was a slight change in the industrial classification between 1947 and 1948, which does not affect the figures given here.

9. The Rates of Return are from Stigler [25], Tables A-36 to A-59, pp. 170–202 and Errata, Table 1, p. 4.

INFLATION AND THE LAG
IN ACCOUNTING PRACTICE
CRITIQUE

Maurice Moonitz

This paper by Mr. Fabricant is an excellent piece of work. It is most valuable in its marshalling of the evidence on the magnitude of the changes in prices that have occurred in the United States in recent decades. Consideration of this evidence does lead one to wonder why we in the field of accounting have lagged so much in recognizing price changes in our practices. Instead of criticizing specific portions of this paper, let me make some comments on three points with respect to "price-level" accounting in general.

GENERAL PRICE-LEVEL RESTATEMENTS AS A "SCALE" ADJUSTMENT

One of the best sections in Mr. Fabricant's paper is the one on "Treatment of Relative Price Changes." It will repay close study and attention because it deals with the precise identification of the quality or characteristic we are trying to measure in making "price-level" restatements. I will suggest, however, that the same point that Mr. Fabricant is making at some length can be made much more compactly by use of some of the recent work on the meaning of "scales" in measurement.[1] When we set out to measure changes in the "general purchasing-power of money," we are trying to measure changes in the "exchange-value of money," that is, the power of the local legal tender to command goods and services in the market. Since we use money (local legal tender) as our unit of measure in accounting, we are in effect trying to allow for changes in the scale of measurement employed. For example, if an index of general purchasing-power rises from 100 to 200, we interpret this as a reduction in the "exchange-value of money" by one-half. The dollar as a measuring unit has shrunk by one-half. When we restate a set of accounts for this effect, and this effect alone, we are making a restatement or transformation from one scale of measurement

---

[1] See for example, Raymond J. Chambers [2, pp. 85–96] and Richard Mattessich [3, pp. 52–74].

153

to another (e.g., from the "dollar of 1965" to the "dollar of 1966"). But if we make this transformation from one scale to another, we are not reflecting any change at all in the dimension (quality) we are measuring. When we transform a man's weight in pounds into his weight in kilograms, the change in numbers is not a change in his weight but is merely a change in the scale we have used to measure that weight. We do not and cannot conclude that his weight has changed just because his weight measured in number of pounds is greater than the number of kilograms, expressing the same "heaviness." The difference between those two numbers has no significance; in fact, should not even be calculated.

The application to our accounting problem can now be made. When we restate accounts expressed in 1965 dollars into 1966 dollars, we are not expressing anything new; we are not reflecting any "change" that has occurred, except in the size of the unit of measurement employed in the "scale" of monetary values we are employing. Therefore, the "difference" in the number (e.g., 1966 dollars versus 1965 dollars) cannot give rise to gain or loss, realized or unrealized. Any gain or loss that may be present will be revealed by a study of "relative price changes," that is to say, changes in the market position of one set of assets at a point in time as compared with the market position of that same set of assets at another point in time.

Someone may object that what I have just said is not applicable to the "monetary assets." But it is. The monetary items should also be restated solely for the "scale" effect, in the same manner as the nonmonetary items. In fact, the distinction between monetary and nonmonetary items should not be drawn until after all elements in the accounts are expressed in terms of units on the same scale, e.g., 1966 dollars. After the "scale adjustment" is made, we should then look at the resultant numbers to ask whether they make sense from the standpoint of financial reporting. Clearly, they will not, with respect to cash balances, because cash is by law worth its face value, no more and no less. Consequently, in a period of inflation, we will show a "loss" on holdings of cash. This aspect of the matter is clear enough with respect to cash. By extension we ordinarily apply the same reasoning to contracts in terms of money (receivables and payables primarily), but we should recognize what we are doing. We are taking the restated (i.e., scale-adjusted) items and reflecting them at their "current cash equivalent" or "net realizable value." How far this process should be carried (e.g., to receivables? foreign bank accounts?) depends on the "realization" rules we are observing. I am pointing out, in effect, that the popular classification of all balance sheet items into "monetary" and "nonmonetary" is an over-simplification at least and, more seriously, leads us into the belief that these are two different kinds of items, when, in fact, they are not. We simply have treated them in the past as if they were. In the near future, I hope to elaborate these remarks somewhat more systematically, but they will have to do for the present.

ADJUSTMENTS ALREADY MADE

Mr. Fabricant wonders why accounting practice has lagged so far behind the record of events. One of the reasons I have heard expressed by some practitioners is that accounting practice may, in fact, already have cverreacted to the distorting effects of changing price-levels. They refer, for one thing, to LIFO inventory pricing. Although this practice was originally introduced in the late 1930's as a reaction to cyclical price movements with respect to specific commodities, it has proved much more useful as a device to reduce reported profits below what they would otherwise be in a period of inflation than under almost any other method of inventory pricing. Similarly, at least since the adoption of the Internal Revenue Code of 1954, we have had extensive use of accelerated depreciation methods. These methods have been adopted, I am told, not because they reflect the history of the depreciating items more accurately than the depreciation methods previously used, but rather because they also, like LIFO, reduce reported profits below what they otherwise would be. If my informants are correct in their assessment of the situation, then a "scale adjustment" for inflation, on top of LIFO and accelerated depreciation, would further reduce reported profits when they may have already been driven below permissible levels of conservative reporting. These practitioners are not enthusiastic about "price-level accounting" unless it is joined with the adoption of more sensible and more realistic valuation practices with respect to inventories and fixed assets. They are more concerned about the suppression of "current values" in present-day reporting than they are about the mixture of "scales of measurement" admittedly present in our accounts. My own view is that ideally we need both. We need to use a uniform scale of measurement in our accounts (i.e., general price-level restatement) and also include more current data in our financial statements (i.e., the effects of specific or relative price movements). From the standpoint of measurement theory, the need for a uniform scale would seem to be paramount, since it is always required for valid comparisons, whether the data to be compared are on a historical basis, a projected basis, or a current market-price basis. From the standpoint of usefulness, "current values" may be more pertinent, since in the short-run, relative price changes can easily swamp the more or less modest changes we have had on an annual basis in the U.S. in the exchange value of money.

THE PSYCHOLOGICAL BARRIER

As a final comment, let me point out that we should not under-estimate the extent of the change required in the thinking habits of businessmen before we can expect enthusiastic acceptance of "price-level accounting." The "money-illusion" is an illusion widely held by businessmen — they do believe that prices change but that the dollar does not (barring perhaps a legal devaluation such as we had in 1933 when we went off the full gold standard). Veblen noted this several decades ago and called it a "tropismatic" reaction, that is, a reaction based on a belief known to be false but acted on as if it were true. After all, prices are quoted in dollars, without specification of the size of those dollars; contracts are expressed in dollars; our accounts are kept in dollars; the businessman's success or failure is expressed in dollars. We cannot expect him to accept either easily or readily the notion that this solid platform under his planning and acting is actually shifting in space, not really anchored too tightly to much of anything. He is much more likely to accept or even advocate the more extended use of "relative" price data than general price-level (scale) adjustments. After all, a shift from "historical costs" to "current values" will merely shift the period in which profits are recognized but will not change the total amount of profit or loss resulting from any set of completed transactions or ventures. Consequently, the battle over "historical" or "current" costs or values is essentially a practical, limited battle over such things as what constitutes prudent conduct with respect to dividends or investment policy or when taxes on income should be calculated or paid. These are important matters, indeed, because of the magnitudes involved; but they do not require a businessman to abandon the underpinnings of all his financial calculations.

If you will examine carefully the cases in which "price-level" accounting has been employed, you will find that in most instances the "scale" adjustment has not been made properly, and that the restated accounts have been made the occasion for adopting even more conservative practices of calculating net income than those hitherto in effect. For example, the Philips Lamp financial statements[2] are often cited as examples of fully-adjusted reports. In fact, they are devices to prevent *relative* price changes from entering into net income and retained earnings, except by way of losses. We are still a far way from acceptance by the business community of the need or desirability of full-blown "scale" adjustments.

---

[2]American Institute of Certified Public Accountants [1, pp. 183–93].

BIBLIOGRAPHY

[1] American Institute of Certified Public Accountants. "Reporting the Financial Effects of Price-Level Changes." *Accounting Research Study No. 6.* New York: American Institute of Certified Public Accountants, Inc., 1963.

[2] Chambers, Raymond J. *Accounting, Evaluation and Economic Behavior.* Englewood Cliffs, New Jersey: Prentice-Hall, Inc., 1966.

[3] Mattessich, Richard. *Accounting and Analytical Methods.* Homewood, Illinois: Richard D. Irwin, Inc., 1964.

INFLATION AND THE LAG IN
ACCOUNTING PRACTICE

CRITIQUE

Paul Rosenfield

THE LAG IN ACCOUNTING PRACTICE

I will comment on issues raised by Professor Fabricant and bring you up-to-date on the Institute's project on general price-level accounting. However, I would first like to discuss the lag in accounting practice to which Professor Fabricant refers.

I can think of several reasons to agree that there has been a lag. Henry Sweeney's seminal book on general price-level accounting, *Stabilized Accounting* [9], was published 33 years ago. Professor Fabricant presented today many of the ideas he expressed 19 years ago in his papers "Business Costs and Business Income Under Changing Price Levels" [4] and "The Varied Impact of Inflation in the Calculation of Business Income" [5]. And the American Institute of CPAs announced its project on general price-level accounting in 1961 — eight years ago.

A couple of reasons perhaps explain why accountants have not moved very fast in this area. First, practitioners may have been confused on what to do about price changes because of the disagreement among writers on the subject, whose recommendations have been all over the map. It is understandable that practicing accountants did not know exactly what to do, if anything. Second, I am sure that there has been widespread feeling, which I shared when I was in public practice, that changes in the general price level experienced in the United States have not been large enough to hurt too much — that moderate inflation results in moderate or perhaps even immaterial differences between unrestated and restated financial statement amounts. The feeling has therefore been that it is not important to learn the theory and practice of general price-level accounting because there are enough other, more important problems.

Accounting practice cannot lead the way in this area as it has in many areas; accountants should have the way pointed out to them. The Accounting Principles Board now seems to be willing to take the lead. Of course, the Board is not being pushed into action in this area as it is in many other areas. Perhaps that is one reason why the Board's project has been on the back burner for eight years. But the fire has been on and the pot has been simmering; I can say that things have been happening.

FIELD TEST

One of the things that has happened is a field test of general price-level accounting sponsored by the Accounting Principles Board. Eighteen companies agreed to use a research draft of a proposed APB pronouncement on the subject as a guide to restate their statements for one or two years. Indexes of the inflation actually experienced in the United States in recent years were used. I applied the restatement procedures for one of the companies and can report that it is a very educational experience.

Many of the participants in the test were surprised by the magnitude of the differences between restated and historical-dollar figures. They apparently had the same idea in advance that I had in public practice, that restatement would not make much difference. The results of the test,[1] however, included a difference between unrestated net income and restated net income of 31% for one company, included no difference for another company, and included just about every percentage in between for the other participants. Thus, some of the differences were many times the rate of inflation in any particular recent year.

Two reasons for the ballooning effect of restatement — for magnification of the annual rates of inflation — are easily identified. First, restatement of amounts for assets purchased in the past involves the cumulative compound inflation for all the years since the assets were purchased and not just for the inflation in one year. The effect of a 2% inflation rate on depreciation expense will therefore be more than 20% in 10 years. Second, restatement by a small percentage of large income statement items such as sales or the opening inventory component of cost of goods sold can result in a difference that is a large percentage of net income. Furthermore, restated statements of income include an item, general price-level gain or loss on monetary items, which does not appear in conventional statements of income. In two of the companies the general price-level gain was about 50% of the restated net income.

Before the test results were in, I was rash enough to say that I thought restated net income would be lower than before restatement in every case. I believe that is a common assumption. The results did not turn out that way. Four of the companies showed greater

---

[1] See Paul Rosenfield [6, pp. 45–50].

restated profit — 30% greater for one company — than historical-dollar profit. These results were caused by large general price-level gains on monetary items not fully offset by higher expense charges. The fact that, for some of the companies, restated net income is higher than before restatement and lower for others further magnifies the change in comparisons between companies caused by restatement.

Although I recognize that results of an 18-company test are not necessarily statistically valid, I nevertheless conclude that the test demonstrates that significant differences can result from restating for moderate inflation. I believe the differences cannot be ignored, and accountants should be encouraged by the test to take a more active interest concerning the meaning of the differences. The implicit excuse that the size of the differences is probably so small that the subject is unimportant is certainly weakened by the test results. I doubt that we will have a stampede to publish restated statements in the near future, but if the Accounting Principles Board does issue a pronouncement putting its weight behind the idea,[2] I think that weight, coupled with the results of the test, will encourage more companies to present restated data than in the past.

PROFESSOR FABRICANT'S PAPER

I generally agree with the broad outlines of Professor Fabricant's proposal. However, there are a couple of points I would take issue with in his paper.

Professor Fabricant states that the Gross National Product Implicit Price Deflator (GNP Deflator) is the best index.[3] Conceptually I disagree with this. It is my position — and I have been influenced by the arguments of Sweeney,[4] Chambers,[5] and of our co-chairman, Bob Sterling[6] — that prices of producers' goods should be excluded and that an index confined to consumers' goods should be used. I am not contending that the Consumers Price Index of the United States Department of Labor is necessarily superior now, but merely that an index of the prices of all consumers' goods and services is the conceptually sound index. The issue is complicated, so I will not give you my arguments or repeat those of others, but I do not think that the weight of argument is in favor of the GNP Deflator.

---

[2]Since the original presentation of the paper, the Accounting Principles Board issued Statement No. 3, "Financial Statements Restated for General Price-Level Changes," in June, 1969 [1].

[3]The use of the GNP Deflator is recommended in Sprouse and Moonitz [7] and in [1].
[4]Henry W. Sweeney [9, p. 4].
[5]Raymond J. Chambers [3, p. 229].
[6]Robert R. Sterling [8, pp. 340–41].

Professor Fabricant said that whether restated financial statements are presented in current dollars or in base year dollars is not too important. I believe the choice makes a considerable difference. There are important arguments in favor of each method. For example, restatements do not have to be updated for comparison with restatements in succeeding years if base year dollars are used. On the other hand, financial statement information is used to make decisions based on current prices and other current indicators. Furthermore, it is important that all companies use the same dollar, whether it is a specified base year or current dollars. The Board is currently considering this question and seems to favor current dollars.[7]

OTHER ISSUES

I might mention other issues in general price-level accounting which are currently of concern to us in the accounting research division. The first is the question as to where to draw the line between monetary and nonmonetary items. For example, is foreign currency a monetary or nonmonetary item? My position is that it is nonmonetary.[8] I will not state the argument here but merely say that it is a good example of an unsolved question.

A second question is whether we should support general price-level accounting although it solves only part of the problem of changing prices. General price-level accounting does not get at the problem of relative changes in prices, but merely the problem of changes in the general level of prices. My answer would be that the profession should now support the partial solution recommended by Professor Fabricant and *Accounting Research Study No. 6* [2]. Solution to the price-relative problem can be achieved gradually; accounting for some items, such as marketable securities, can be switched from cost to current value while cost is retained for other items. General price-level restatement, on the other hand, should be done comprehensively, with all items stated in terms of dollars of the same general purchasing power, or it should not be done at all. Piecemeal solution to the general price-level problem, which has been advocated in the past, should be avoided; it results in reporting only part of the effects of inflation on an enterprise and can give a biased view.

A third issue, one that has had us going around in circles, is whether statements of foreign operations that are to be combined or

---

[7]The Board adopted current dollars in Statement No. 3 (see paragraph 32 of [1]). This issue is one of several discussed in forthcoming research papers to be issued by the Accounting Research Division of the American Institute of Certified Public Accountants.

[8]This issue is discussed in a forthcoming research paper. See footnote 7.

consolidated with statements of a U. S. parent company should be restated using an index of the general price-level in the foreign country or using the U. S. general price-level index. In other words, should statements first be restated and then translated, or first translated and then restated? Intuitively, the first restate, then translate solution seems appealing because the subsidiary is operating in the midst of the foreign inflation. I nevertheless believe that all restatement for U. S. dollar consolidated statements should use only the U. S. general price-level index. I am working at trying to prove my point.[9]

Companies following the recommendation of *ARS 6* [2] will publish two sets of statements — historical-dollar statements and general price-level statements. This is a fourth problem, because a company will report two different amounts for net income which may both be reported in the press. The two amounts are presented on different bases, of course, and do not conflict, but will a small shareholder of the company know this? Will it add confusion? I am not sure. One thing I know is that we cannot get the general price-level statements to be the only statements now. That would be absolutely impossible, considering the educational job that would be required for both accountants and users, to cite just one problem. The only practical way to get general price-level statements now is as supplementary statements. I therefore think we should advocate two sets of statements and work to reduce any possible confusion by detailed descriptions attached to the statements.

Governmental agencies have not encouraged companies to publish general price-level information. One reason perhaps has been that accountants have not formally agreed to and recommended the use of a uniform, workable method. Another may be that presentation of this information may cause administrative problems to increase (although use of a single published index series should not present objectivity problems). And the fact that the federal government benefits from inflation which is not reflected in the Internal Revenue Code and which lightens the burden of the national debt (which is well known to economists) might become more apparent to all. I do not think, however, that we should be influenced one way or another by side issues such as these. Our objective as accountants should be to present information useful to investors and other readers of financial statements.

I believe that general price-level statements present useful information and that proposals such as those by Professor Fabricant and in *ARS 6* should therefore be supported.

---

[9]This issue is discussed in a forthcoming research paper. See footnote 8.

BIBLIOGRAPHY

[1] American Institute of Certified Public Accountants. "Financial Statements Restated for General Price-Level Changes." Statement by
the Accounting Principles Board No. 3. New York: American
Institute of Certified Public Accountants, June, 1969.

[2] American Institute of Certified Public Accountants. "Reporting the
Financial Effects of Price Level Changes." *Accounting Research
Study No. 6.* New York: American Institute of Certified Public
Accountants, 1963.

[3] Chambers, Raymond J. *Accounting, Evaluation and Economic Behavior.* Englewood Cliffs, N. J.: Prentice-Hall, Inc., 1966.

[4] Fabricant, Solomon. "Business Costs and Business Income Under
Changing Price Levels," in Study Group on Business Income. *Five
Monographs on Business Income.* New York: American Institute
of Accountants, 1950.

[5] ——————. "The Varied Impact of Inflation on the Calculation of
Business Income," in Study Group on Business Income. *Five
Monographs on Business Income.* New York: American Institute
of Accountants, 1950.

[6] Rosenfield, Paul. "Accounting for Inflation — A Field Test." *The
Journal of Accountancy,* Vol. CXXVII, No. 6 (June, 1969),
pp. 45–50.

[7] Sprouse, Robert T., and Maurice Moonitz. *A Tentative Set of Broad
Accounting Principles for Business Enterprises.* Accounting Research Study No. 3. American Institute of Certified Public Accountants, 1962.

[8] Sterling, Robert R. *Theory of the Measurement of Enterprise Income.*
Lawrence, Kansas: The University Press of Kansas, 1970.

[9] Sweeney, Henry W. *Stabilized Accounting.* New York: Holt, Rinehart
and Winston, Inc., 1964. First published by Harper & Brothers, 1936.

RETURN ON INVESTMENT: THE CONTINUING CONFUSION AMONG DISPARATE MEASURES

Ezra Solomon*

My first obligation is to apologize to my two critics, Professors Gordon and Staubus, for not having sent them my paper. Fortunately, both men have themselves done a great deal of pioneering work on the topic I have been asked to present. This reduces my feelings of guilt if not the guilt itself.

The concept "return on investment" or "profitability" is central to much of financial analysis. It is used as a summary measure for at least three purposes:

1. as a measure of the investment worth of a proposed investment outlay,
2. as a measure of the on-going performance of previously invested capital funds, and
3. as a standard of the fair or expected performance from capital investment.

Because analysis is essentially a process of comparing these measures against one another, it is crucial that the measures themselves should be consonant or congruent. Unfortunately, this is not the case. These measures reflect basically different concepts and scales of measurements even though all of the measures bear the same label, "rate of return on investment," and all are expressed in what appears to be a common unit of account, percent per annum. In other words, observed variations in the numerical size of these measures are not just alternative estimates of a common concept; rather, they represent varying estimates of different concepts, all of which are paraded under a single label. Needless to say, this state of affairs can and does lead to considerable confusion.

Some of the variations in concept are trivial. For example, rates of return can be computed either on a pre-tax or on a post-tax basis. Also, rates may refer either to total investment (including debt and

*I am grateful to Nester Gonzalez for his help in preparing the written draft of this manuscript.

equity capital) or only to the equity component. The numerical differences resulting from these two alternative sets of bases may be large, but the consequences are trivial because the differences are so obvious they rarely lead to any confusion at the analytical level.

We shall discuss two non-trivial variants which are less obvious and which therefore can and do lead to confusion in any analysis using an intercomparison among disparate measures. These are:

1. the distinction between true yield and book yield, and
2. the distinction between the real rates and nominal rates.

The analysis which follows explores each of these two important distinctions separately. In order to keep the exposition manageable, the two other distinctions mentioned earlier will be ignored. In other words, throughout this paper I will assume for purposes of analysis that there are no income taxes, and that all investments are financed entirely by equity.

BOOK YIELD AND TRUE YIELD

The first source of potential confusion is that profitability can be defined and measured in two different ways. The first, and more fundamental way, is to define profitability as that rate of interest or discount which equates the value of net cash inflows generated by an investment outlay to the value of the outlay itself. This measure is known by various names, such as "the effective yield," "the true yield," and the "discounted cash flow (DCF) yield."

A second way, which represents a shortcut process for measuring the rate of profitability, defines it as the ratio of net book income generated by an investment outlay to the average net book value of the investment outlay over its productive life. I will refer to this as the book yield.

Confusion can arise because:

(a) the book yield is not an unbiased measure of the true yield, and

(b) the extent of the bias varies from one situation to another.

TRUE YIELD

Ignoring income taxes, the true yield from any investment outlay is determined exclusively by the configuration of the net cash inflows generated by that outlay.[1] Configuration in this context is a compound

---

[1]The distinction between funds and cash is ignored for purposes of exposition. Net cash inflow in any period is equal to the total cash revenues received in the period less those cash expenditures in the period which are required to produce these specific revenues. Net cash inflows have also been referred to as quasi-rents.

concept which includes the size, timing, pattern, and duration of net cash inflows. The size or scale element can be eliminated by reasoning in terms of net cash inflows *per unit of investment*, and this procedure will be used in much of the analysis which follows.

We know all too little about the configuration of inflows from specific non-financial investments, but we do know that they differ widely from one investment to the next. Some of the major factors influencing configuration are outlined below.

Construction time lags. — Some forms of capital, e.g., a utility plant, take time to build. Others, e.g., a truck, can be put into service immediately.

Development time lags. — For some forms of capital, it is useful to think in terms of a development lag rather than a construction lag. Exploring for and establishing a producing oil or gas well, for example, is an investment involving a long development lag. The time required to get a newly constructed or acquired steel mill, or computer, to capacity-level operations is another such example. In contrast, our earlier example of a truck is an investment which suffers neither a construction nor a developmental time lag.

Market time lags. — Even after their full physical capability is achieved, some forms of capital investment might suffer a further lag before full market penetration is achieved. This is especially true of new products and of products being extended to new markets.

The time pattern of benefits. — The example just cited of new products would probably show a rising pattern of net cash inflows over time. In contrast, many forms of investment, particularly those associated with new models of old products or fashion products, probably generate decaying net cash inflows. Some examples of such products are new editions of college textbooks, new models of automobiles, and new versions of soap or cosmetic products.

The duration of benefits. — Some investments produce cash inflows of long duration, e.g., apartment houses and oil wells. For others the duration is relatively short.

The ratio of salvage value to initial outlay. — The final element in the configuration of net cash inflows is the scrap or salvage value of the investment. For some investments it is relatively high, e.g., a bond, a building, working capital, or real estate. For others the ratio of salvage value to initial investment is negligible or even negative, if salvage involves net removal costs.

Obviously, given all of these dimensions, the number of possible configurations is infinite, even if we ignore price level changes.

Indeed, for any given true yield, an infinite number of configurations are compatible.

Algebraically we have:

$$\sum_{t=1}^{n} F_t / (1 + r)^t = 1 \qquad\qquad (1)$$

where F_t = net cash inflow (including salvage value) at time t,
  n = the productive life of each investment,
  r = the true yield, and
  1 = the unit investment at time $t = 0$.

In the equation above, an infinite number of configurations for F_t, for any given value of r, are possible.

But given the configuration of net cash inflows, there is only one true yield, r* for any given investment.[2] If a company holds *only* this given or assumed type of investment in its portfolio, the true yield earned by the company, which we will denote with the symbol R*, will be equal to the project's true yield r*. This statement is correct regardless of the accounting procedures used for bookkeeping purposes (we are assuming that income taxes do not exist) and regardless of the pace at which such investments are acquired over time.

BOOK YIELD

The book yield on an investment, or for a company, is measured through a process which is quite distinct from that shown in Equation 1.

For situations in which salvage value is zero, the average book yield for a particular project or investment, denoted by b*, is given by Equation 2 below.

$$b^* = (1/K^*)\left[\sum_{t=1}^{n} F_t / n - 1/n \right] \qquad\qquad (2)$$

In Equation 2, the denominator K* is the average net book value of the investment over its productive life span.

---

[2]For investments made at a point in time t_o this statement is true without qualification. For investments which require outlays over some period of time, investment should be defined as the *time-adjusted* value of those outlays, i.e., the equivalent point outlay at time t_o. The appropriate rate for this time adjustment is the company's cost of capital during the outlay phase of the investment. In other words, the true yield being discussed is not exactly the same thing as the "internal rate of return," if the latter is defined as that rate which equates net inflows over time to net outlays over time. The internal rate of return, so defined, can have several values for any given inflow configuration.

The numerator of the investment is simply the lifetime net income generated by the unit investment (total lifetime net cash flow less lifetime capital expensing or depreciation) reduced to a per annum basis.

Any company which invests the same amount each year to acquire a series of identical investments, each of which produces an average lifetime book yield equal to b*, will also show a company book yield, denoted by B*, which is equal to b*, after n successive years of such investment (assuming, of course, that depreciation methods are unchanged).

THE RELATIONSHIP OF B* TO R*

The company book yield B* may or may not be equal to company true yield R*. The difference between B* and R* varies from situation to situation. It can be negative, zero, or positive, and the difference may vary from very small to very large. The reasons for these variations have been explored fairly thoroughly in recent years (see Bibliography) and these reasons need not be repeated here. A summary of the major sources of difference between B* and R* will suffice.

Essentially, three sets of causes accounting for most of the potential difference between B* and R* are worth noting. We explain below.

Accounting practices. — For any given configuration of net cash inflows F_t the project book yield b* is not an unbiased measure of the project true yield r*. This is due to the fact that r* is exclusively determined by the given configuration F_t, and is not influenced by the accounting procedures or practices used. In contrast, the book yield b* is heavily influenced by accounting practices. The pace at which each investment outlay is charged off over time, either through the immediate expensing of a portion of the investment outlay or through the subsequent formula used for depreciating capitalized investment outlay, has no influence on the numerator of the project book yield equation (Equation 2). It does, however, have a profound influence on the denominator of this equation, i.e., on the value of K*. For the unit investment case, K* may vary from a low of zero, for a 100% expensing policy, to a high of 1, for a policy in which all investment is fully capitalized for book purposes and written off only when scrapped. Thus, the book yield b* can range from a value well below r* (in the latter situation) to as high as infinity (in the former situation).[3]

---

[3]For a level cash flow configuration it has long been known that a full capitalization, sinking fund depreciation procedure (with the rate r* built into the sinking fund calculation) will produce a book yield b* just equal to r*.

It has also been shown that a full capitalization, straight-line depreciation formula will produce a correct b* for cash inflows which decay linearly. See Anton [1], Carlson [3], Edwards [4], Hotelling [8], Jones [10], and NAA [12].

In the real world, the observed range for the book yield b* associated with any given configuration may not extend to these extremes, but it is nonetheless very wide.

Configuration. — The project book yield measured b* is highly sensitive to accounting practices, whereas the project true yield measure r* is not. But even if accounting practices are held constant, b* would be an erratically biased measure of r* for another reason. Namely, that r* is sensitive to changes in net cash flow configuration (which is as it should be) but b* is not. In short, the way in which b* is defined ignores the timing of net cash inflows from each investment; rather, it depends primarily on fairly fixed conventions. Thus, large portions of some forms of investment outlays are written off instantaneously as "expenses," regardless of the expected duration of their contribution to cash flows. Some examples of this practice are research and development outlays, advertising outlays having a larger than one-period effect, exploration and exploratory drilling expenditures, and many types of expenditures for tooling.

Furthermore, that portion of investment which is capitalized for book purposes is written down at some conventional pace, e.g., straight-line or sum-of-the-years'-digits, which may, or more frequently may not, fit the actual pace at which the cash-flow generating power of the asset actually declines. Apart from some conscious attempt to vary the "expected life" used in a depreciation formula in accord with the asset's probable life, the same set of procedures are used for many types of configurations. In most situations this will not be the "correct" one because one, and only one, set of admissible write-off procedures fits any given configuration. This is the set which over the life of a given investment produces a value for net book capital that is always just equal to the present value (at the project true yield r*) of the yet to be recovered net cash inflows from that investment.

If this condition is fulfilled, the project book yield b* will be equal to the project true yield r*. A corollary of this condition is that the year-by-year measure of the project's book yield, denoted by b_t^* will be constant and equal to the project's average book yield over its life span.[4]

In general, these conditions are not fulfilled. The project's year-by-year book yield b_t^* *varies* over time, and the average lifetime book yield b* is not equal to the underlying true yield r*. It is possible to envision an infinite number of configurations, each of which produces a given constant true yield r*. If accounting procedures are held constant in measuring the book yield for each of these configurations, the answers obtained for b* would vary over a wide range because the

[4]See Anton [1], Carlson [3], Edwards [4], Hotelling [8], Jones [10], or NAA [12].

numerator of the book-yield equation varies although the denominator is constant.

It is also possible to envision the opposite situation: an infinite number of configurations, each of which has a *different* true yield, but which nonetheless appear to have a common constant "return on investment" when measured on a book-yield basis. In summary, the project book yield b* is rarely an unbiased measure of the project's true yield r*. In general, it is a biased measure of r* and the direction and extent of the bias can vary over a considerable range.

Growth. — Growth, in the present context, is defined as the change in the pace at which a company makes investment outlays over time. In the absence of price level changes, a steady annual outlay of investment funds each year in similar projects (with given configuration of n years duration) will lead, after n years, to a steady no-growth state in which the value of all variables stabilize. This includes cash inflow, income, and gross book value. Positive growth is defined as a situation in which the company increases investment outlays each year, and the rate of growth g is equal to the rate at which annual outlays increase over time. Decay (negative growth) exists when the opposite occurs, i.e., constantly decreasing investment outlays.

The rate of growth has no effect on either the project true yield r* (which is determined by the assumed configuration) or on the project book yield b* (which is determined jointly by the configuration and whatever set of accounting practices are assumed). Nor does the rate of growth influence R*, the true yield being earned by the company, because if each investment yields r*, then it follows that the company's portfolio of investments must also be yielding r*. In short R* = r* and the pace at which investments are acquired affects neither.

However, this equality between project true yield and company true yield does *not* hold for the book yield measures b* and B* except under two very specific conditions. These are:

(1)   if b_t^* is constant, or
(2)   if the growth rate g is equal to r*.

These two conditions are analyzed in the following section.

THE EFFECT OF GROWTH ON B*

If b* is constant over time, then B* will be equal to b* for all growth rates. The reasons for this statement are fairly straightforward. The company book yield in any period T (where T is larger than n) is a weighted average of that year's book yield for each of the n individual projects held in the portfolio. Growth itself does not affect the book yield on each individual project. It does affect the relative weight which each project has in the overall portfolio. Positive growth increases the weights of the more recently acquired (and hence larger) investments relative to the weights of the older (and hence smaller) investments. Negative growth has the opposite effect.

Now if b_t^* is constant over each year of the project's life, i.e., in any given year T, it is the same for "old" as opposed to "new" investments; any set of relative weights will give the same answer for the weighted average of project book yields. Thus changes in the growth rate of outlays, which change the relative weights of the various vintages of investment held at time T, have no effect on the value of B*.

But if the condition that b* is constant over time does not hold in the first place, then the equality of B* and b* breaks down. At any time T, the older vintages of investment yield a different period book yield than do the newer vintages (even though both vintages have a common lifetime book yield b*). In this situation, the relative weights of the different vintages within the company's portfolio do affect the company's overall book yield B* because B* is equal to the *weighted average* of the individual project book yields in that particular year. Thus B* will not be equal to b* for growth rates other than zero.

Since R* = r* for any growth rate, the difference between B* and R* (the relative bias in the company book yield measure) can be thought of as a complex result of two separate factors:

(1) the basic difference between b* and r*, and
(2) the growth-induced difference between b* and B*.

Fortunately, these two errors tend to be offsetting ones when growth is positive.[5] If b* is larger than r* (error one is positive) then *positive* growth drives B* below b* (error number two is negative). If b* is smaller than r* (error one is negative) then *positive* growth increases B* relative to b* (error number two is positive).

There is one growth rate at which the two errors just cancel, giving us a situation in which the company book yield B* is an unbiased measure of R* regardless of any basic bias in the project book yield b*. This occurs when the growth rate in investment outlays g is just equal to the project true yield r*.

A short, and partly intuitive "proof" of this follows. By definition we have:

$$B_t^* = \frac{F_t^* - D_t^*}{K_t^*} \tag{3}$$

---

[5]Fortunately, because growth is generally positive. Negative growth or decay magnifies the joint result of the two errors.

$$g = \frac{I_t^* - D_t^*}{K_t^*} \qquad\qquad (4)$$

The first equation says that the company's book yield (in period t) is equal to income in that period (defined as net cash flow in the period *less* write-off of capital in the period) divided by net book value of the existing stock of investments held in period t.

The second equation says that the company's growth rate g can be measured by the rate of change in its stock of net book capital. (At any steady growth rate, new investment outlays and the net book value of investments held will both increase at the same rate.)

If a company is growing exactly at a rate $g = r^*$ (or R^*), it must be continuously investing an amount just equal to the net cash flow being generated. The easiest way to see that this must be true is to think in terms of a barrel of whisky which improves in value with time. The true rate of return (r^*) earned by holding the barrel another year is equal to the growth in the value of the barrel g if, and only if, one neither adds to, nor subtracts from its contents! In other words, the $g = r^*$ condition requires the exact "reinvestment" of the entire cash flow.

Thus if $g = r^*$ we know that $I_t = F_t$ and we can see from equations (3) and (4) that $g = B_t^*$. Hence if $g = r^*$, we have $g = B_t^*$ and $B_t^* = r^*$.

REAL RATES AND NOMINAL RATES

Thus far my analysis has ignored price-level changes and their effect on measures of profitability. It is time now to extend the inquiry to include such changes. However, I will confine myself to the simplest of inflationary situations — namely, one in which all price-indexes change together at some common rate p.

The introduction of $p \neq 0$ makes it necessary to distinguish two new dimensions of any rate measure: a *real* rate (the rate that would prevail in the absence of price changes) and the *nominal* or money rate (the rate that actually prevails when $p \neq 0$). This distinction applies both to the true yield measure and the book yield type of measure.

The effect of $p > 0$ on the true rate is fairly straightforward. If the real true rate is r^* (expressed in decimal notation) the nominal or money true rate is given by $[(1 + r^*)(1 + p) - 1]$. The effects of $p > 0$ on the money book yield are more complex. The nominal project book yield will also rise relative to the real project book yield as the cash flows over the project's life are inflated by a rising price level (whereas the net book value for the project is left unchanged). However, there is no simple relationship between the nominal rate and the real rate in the case of the project book yield measure, i.e., the nominal project book yield is *not* necessarily equal to $[(1 + b^*)(1 + p) - 1]$. In general, if b^* is larger than r^* (in the absence of inflation), inflation will increase the relative discrepancy between the nominal project book yield and the nominal true yield.

The introduction of real growth in addition to purely inflationary growth has the same *kind* of effect in the inflationary situation as it does when price levels are constant. Growth drives the nominal company book yield toward the nominal company true yield and equality between them is achieved at a growth rate equal to the true yield.

In general, however, the presence of inflation injects a further element of difficulty to the task of interpreting the relationship between any observable nominal book yield and the underlying true yield actually being generated by a company.

Inflation (or deflation) also creates difficulties for anyone trying to measure the "cost of capital" — defined as the warranted or fair rate of profitability against which prospective or on-going investment performance is to be assayed. In the absence of inflation (and inflationary expectations), there are only *two* basic ways of estimating such a "fair" rate for capital usage. One way is to look at past or recent book yield data in comparable industries or companies. The other is to look to the DCF or true yield which investors appear to expect on the market values that they are willing to pay for comparable securities. The answers provided by these two methods will be different — primarily because the former is a book yield measure whereas the latter is a true yield measure. But this confusion can be handled with the techniques discussed thus far.

Inflation and inflationary or deflationary expectations introduce a whole new range of problems. With price stability, all of the various *approaches* to the estimation of a DCF cost of capital number yield identical or similar results. This is no longer true with inflation and the possibility of further confusion grows rapidly.

DCF COST OF CAPITAL MODELS

Essentially there are four approaches to the estimation of market-based DCF cost of capital measure, which will be denoted by the letter C. These are:

1. $C = \dfrac{E}{P}$ (the earnings-price ratio),

2. $C = \dfrac{D}{P} + g$ (dividend yield plus the growth rate of dividends),

3. $C = \dfrac{F}{P} - z$ (cash flow yield *less* the expected decay rate of cash flows), and

4. $C = \dfrac{D + \Delta P}{P}$ (dividend yield plus average market price appreciation).

All four approaches will yield similar, if not identical results only if four conditions are fulfilled:

(a) the price level has been and is expected to be constant,

(b) the industry being observed is not expected to have opportunities to invest funds at an average true yield higher than the rate C,

(c) if earnings are correctly defined, i.e., the amounts set aside from cash flow in computing earnings are just sufficient, when reinvested, to maintain the existing net cash flow from the existing fund of assets, and

(d) if capital market prices accurately reflect values.

Under such conditions, one can equate market prices either to decaying future cash flows or to growing future dividends, or to a constant stream of earnings and get similar results for the capitalization rate C. Also, market values grow in line with dividends so that the fourth approach also provides an answer that is in line with the first three. The degree to which such an equality of results from alternative approaches actually exists is not crucial for my present purpose. The point is that the existence of actual or expected inflation or deflation will definitely drive these four estimates widely apart. The reason for this is that the four approaches are no longer measures of the same underlying concept; some measure a "real" rate, others measure a "nominal rate," and some measure a complex hybrid of the two.

The Earnings-Price Ratio. — In inflationary situations the ratio of current earnings to market price, if it measures any *rate* at all, must be measuring a real rate. This is so because the $\dfrac{E}{P}$ ratio measures a capitalization rate only if the future flow of earnings is a perpetual, level stream. But if inflation is expected, nominal earnings will not be a level stream. Therefore, the measure must refer to *real* earnings and is therefore a real rate or an estimate of one.

The dividend rate plus average future market appreciation rate. — This measure is wholly nominal and the rate it estimates is therefore also nominal.

The dividend-cum-growth rate. — This measure, as well as the cash flow less decay rate, can reflect varying degrees of nominality depending on the empirical basis from which the estimates for g or z are derived. If the future growth rate used in the measure itself assumes inflation, the resulting estimate is essentially nominal. If on the other hand, the estimates for g or z are based on *real* or *physical* data the estimate is essentially a real rate.

The book yield ratio. — This is a nominal rather than a real rate in the absence of any revaluation of book assets. But unlike the other nominal rates, it reflects past rather then expected inflation.

The failure to distinguish between real, nominal or "hybrid" rates can lead to considerable confusion. Thus, in a recent regulatory rate hearing, the estimates put forward for "fair rate of return on equity" ranged from a low of 6.5 percent (based on the earnings-price approach) to a high of 15.0 percent (by a witness who used comparable book yields based on recent data), with several estimates in between based on the dividend plus growth formula in which the growth term itself was assumed sometimes to be equal to future *real* growth in physical sales and sometimes to past *nominal* growth. Such a range clearly reflects more than simple estimating differences; yet nowhere was the issue of real vs. nominal rates given serious consideration.

SUMMARY

Let me summarize the potential confusions which can arise from the mixing of disparate rates in any intercomparison.

1. Observable book-yields may not be directly comparable with one another, and when configurations, accounting practices, and growth rates differ widely, such direct comparisons can be seriously misleading. This is true in comparisons among divisions of a single company and among companies within an industry, as well as among different industries.

2. True yields may not be commensurate with book yields. The practice of measuring the expected performance of a new investment on a true yield or DCF basis and of trying to relate such an ex-ante true yield with an ex-post book yield, either for post-audit purposes or for the purpose of making the investment decision, may be misleading.

3. Finally, rates that are basically real rates should not be intercompared against rates that are basically nominal rates.

Return on investment is a useful, and probably an essential, tool of thought, but its use for analytical purposes requires a great deal more care than it has received.

BIBLIOGRAPHY

[1] Anton, Hector R. "Depreciation, Cost Allocation and Investment Decisions." *Accounting Research,* Vol. 7, No. 2 (April, 1956), pp. 117–34.

[2] Bierman, Harold, Jr. "Depreciable Assets-Timing of Expense Recognition." *Accounting Review,* Vol. XXXVI, No. 4 (October, 1961), pp. 613–18.

[3] Carlson, Robert S. "Measuring Period Profitability: Book Yield vs. True Yield." Unpublished Ph.D. dissertation, Stanford University, 1964.

[4] Edwards, Edgar O., and Phillip W. Bell. *The Theory and Measurement of Business Income.* Berkeley, California: The University of California Press, 1961.

[5] Gordon, Myron J. "Depreciation Allowances, Replacement and Growth: A Comment." *American Economic Review,* Vol. XLIII, No. 4, Part 1 (September, 1953), pp. 609–14.

[6] —————— . "The Payoff Period and the Rate of Profit." *The Management of Corporate Capital,* edited by Ezra Solomon. New York: The Macmillan Co. — Free Press, 1959, pp. 48–55.

[7] Harcourt, G. C. "The Accountant in a Golden Age." *Oxford Economic Papers* (New Series), Vol. XVII, No. 1 (March, 1965), pp. 66–80.

[8] Hotelling, Harold. "A General Mathematical Theory of Depreciation." *Journal of the American Statistical Association,* Vol. XX, No. 150 (September, 1925), pp. 340–53.

[9] Johnson, Orace. "Two General Concepts of Depreciation." *Journal of Accounting Research,* Vol. VI, No. 1 (Spring, 1968), pp. 29–37.

[10] Jones, Ralph C. *Effects of Price Level Changes on Business Income, Capital and Taxes.* American Accounting Association, 1956.

[11] Laya, Jaime C. "A Cash-Flow Model for Rate of Return." Unpublished Ph.D. dissertation, Stanford University, 1965.

[12] National Association of Accountants. *Return on Investment as a Guide to Management Decisions.* Research Report No. 35. New York: National Association of Accountants, 1959.

[13] Solomon, Ezra. "The Variation Between True Yield and Book Rate of Return in the Oil and Gas Producing Industry." Testimony, Federal Power Commission, Area Rate Proceedings AR61–1, 1961.

[14] —————— . "Systematic Errors in Book Rates of Return." Paper presented at the 38th Annual Meeting of the Society of Petroleum Engineers, 1963.

[15] Solomon, Ezra, and Jaime C. Laya. "Measurement of Company Profitability: Some Systematic Errors in the Accounting Rate of Return." *Financial Research and Management Decisions,* edited by Alexander A. Robichek. New York: John Wiley & Sons, Inc., 1967.

[16] Vatter, William J. "Income Models, Book Yield, and Rate of Return." *Accounting Review,* Vol. XLI, No. 4 (October, 1966), pp. 681–698.

[17] Wright, F. K. "Towards a General Theory of Depreciation." *Journal of Accounting Research,* Vol. 2, No. 1 (Spring, 1964), pp. 80–90.

RETURN ON INVESTMENT: THE CONTINUING CONFUSION AMONG DISPARATE MEASURES

CRITIQUE

Myron J. Gordon

About fifteen years ago a corporate controller told me that he was reluctant to use the DCF or true yield method of evaluating the profitability of investment proposals on the following grounds. Since management's performance is evaluated on the basis of financial statement data, among which earnings and return on equity are the most important statistics, our plans and projections culminate in one and five year financial statement budgets. To incorporate the influence of our investment plan in our earnings budget, we want to use a measure of profitability for the investment budget that is compatible with the measure of profitability for the company as a whole. Clearly, we cannot use DCF in our company financial statements, and we are, therefore, reluctant to use it in calculating the profitability of our capital expenditures.

I saw some merit in the controller's reasoning, thought about the problem, could not figure out a solution and forgot about it. However, Professor Solomon refuses to close his eyes to a problem simply because no solution is evident. He has reminded us quite forcefully that equality between the accounting and the DCF or true rate of return for a project or for a firm as a whole is an extremely rare coincidence. It is even rarer than his paper suggests. In the section on growth, he stated that B* and R*, the accounting and true rates of return for a firm, will be equal "when the growth rate in investment outlays g is just equal to the project true yield r*." (p. 171). The rates of growth and return on a project or for a firm are, by definition, equal if the two rates are measured in the same way and if (as is assumed) the income is not consumed.[1] Hence, his Eqs. (3) and (4) which are *accounting* measures of return and growth, respectively, are by definition equal. With r* = R*, making the assumption that R* is equal to the accounting measure of g is really assuming

---

[1]If no dividends are paid and no shares are sold, a firm's ownership equity at the end of a period exceeds the amount at the start of the period by a fraction equal to the rate of profit. If profits are reinvested to earn the same rate of return as the initial investment, r and g will remain equal and unchanged over time.

that R* = B* and not finding a situation in which they are equal. In fact, a firm that reinvests all of its income will have a DCF rate of return and growth that are equal, and an accounting rate of return and growth that are equal, but the accounting and DCF rates of return will be equal only under the same coincidence or assumption as when all income is not retained.

What should we do about the difference between the DCF and accounting measures of income and return? Returning to the problem posed by the controller referred to above, we might advise him as follows. Use DCF in selecting among the alternative investment opportunities available to your firm. Then use the cash flows and accounting measures of depreciation on the projects accepted to forecast company earnings and return. The controller may reply, however, that a capital budget selected on the basis of accounting rates of return could be different and it could provide a superior future earnings budget for the firm. The standard reply to this statement (one that I would make) is that at each point in time the DCF budget maximizes the present value of the firm's ownership equity and, therefore, it is optimal. However, this is a true statement only if the information used by the firm in arriving at the DCF yield for each project is available to investors in its common stock. If these investors project the firm's future earnings on the basis of reported accounting earnings, the management cannot afford to ignore the consequences of its capital budget for future accounting earnings.

By calling the DCF yield for a firm its true yield, Professor Solomon suggests strongly that it is superior to the accounting yield. Although he is careful not to suggest that accountants should give up cost as a basis of valuation and income determination, some readers may come to this conclusion. In fact, some academic accountants already have come to this conclusion. It therefore may be advisable to explore briefly the implications of adopting true yield as a basis of financial accounting. Let a firm be formed at the start $t = 1$ with an investment of K_1. The true yield, the discount rate that equates its *expected* future cash flows with K_1, is r_1. If the actual cash flow realized during $t = 1$, F_1 is equal to F_1^1, the latter being expected value of F_1 at the start of $t = 1$, and if the expected cash flow during $t = 2, 3, \ldots, \infty$ did not change over the period, we proceed as follows. For $t = 1$ realized income is $r_1 K_1$, depreciation is $F_1 - r_1 K_1$, and r_1 is the realized yield. The value of the firm becomes $K_2 = K_1 (1 + r_1)$ if no dividends are paid, and $r_2 = r_1$ is the true yield at the start $t = 2$.

However, a state of affairs in which the expectation of future cash flows does not change over time is even more exceptional than agreement between B* and R*. In general $F_1 \neq F_1^1$. Also, $F_t^2 \neq F_t^1$ where

F_t^2 is the cash flow in t expected at the start of $t = 2$. There is no general agreement on the value of F_t^j, $j = 2, 3, \ldots, \infty$ and $t \geqslant j$. An accountant, like anyone else, can estimate the F_t^2, but how does he then determine the income the firm realized during $t = 1$? It certainly is not $r_1 K_1$. If it is to be $r_2 K_2$, how are r_2 and K_2 to be determined? The accountant might reasonably take $K_2 = V_2$, the market value of the firm at start of $t = 2$. V_2 is derived from investor consensus with respect to F_t^2 and the yield they require on the company. Given V_2 and the accountant's estimates of F_t^2 he can produce r_2, the yield an investor who accepts the accountant's estimates of F_t^2 can expect to earn by investing in the firm's stock. However, neither $r_1 K_1$ nor $r_2 V_2$ is the income the firm realized during $t = 1$. The firm's true realized income is the dividend during $t = 1$ plus $V_2 - V_1$. However, a subscription to the *Wall Street Journal* and not the services of a public accountant is all that a company and investors need to arrive at the true realized income and return.

All investors and the many investment advisers available to investors estimate a firm's true yield. Should accountants join the crowd or should they continue reporting cost basis realized income and yield even though they are conceptually different from true realized income and true yield? I have argued elsewhere[2] that accountants provide unique and useful data for arriving at estimates of true yield and other useful information by presenting financial statements with cost as the basis of valuation. What is ridiculous is not their failure to adopt DCF as a basis of valuation but their failure to adapt the cost basis of valuation to the demands of changing times.

The final section of the paper deals with alternative cost of capital measures. A firm's cost of capital is that rate of return on investment which the firm must earn in order to maintain the market value of its common equity, and it therefore depends on how investors value a company's shares. Under the four conditions specified, the four measures of the cost of capital are the same and are correct measures of a firm's cost of capital. The consequences of withdrawing these conditions are extremely complex, and statements about the relation between each of these measures and a firm's cost of capital when these conditions are withdrawn are extremely hazardous. An adequate analysis of the observations made on the subject would make this comment on the paper longer than the paper.

A final thought. Confusion among disparate measures of return on investment may be eliminated or reduced, and Professor Solomon's paper may aid in realizing that goal. However, the continued

---

[2]Myron J. Gordon [1] and [2].

existence of disparate measures of return on investment cannot be eliminated as long as the future remains uncertain and expectations as to the future change over time. In particular, the true yield on an asset or a firm at any point in time must in principle be different from the realized yield. The former is the discount rate that equates the expected future cash flows at a point in time with the firm's cost — market value if cost is opportunity cost. Realized yield can be measured in two ways. One measure is cost based income for the period ending at the point in time divided by the cost based investment at the start of the period. The other measure of realized yield is the dividend plus the increase in market value during the period divided by the market value at the start of the period. These three yield figures are in principle different. The accountant has no particular competence in measuring true yield, and he is not needed to provide the second measure of realized yield. The problem that remains is to define cost based realized yield so as to provide data that is useful in estimating true yield.

BIBLIOGRAPHY

[1] Gordon, Myron J. "An Economist's View of Profit Measurement." *Profits in the Modern Economy,* edited by Harold W. Stevenson and J. Russell Nelson. Minneapolis: University of Minnesota Press, 1967.
[2] Gordon, Myron J. "Postulates, Principles and Research in Accounting." *Accounting Review,* Vol. XXXIX, No. 2 (April, 1964), pp. 251–63.

RETURN ON INVESTMENT: THE CONTINUING CONFUSION AMONG DISPARATE MEASURES

CRITIQUE

George J. Staubus

The gist of Professor Solomon's argument in the present paper and others[1] is that current accounting practices do not result in a financial statement rate of return that is a good surrogate for the "true yield" on invested capital. This complaint is of considerable concern to accountants because it represents dissatisfaction with a major set of accounting outputs and implies weaknesses in the basic measurement system through which those outputs are processed. Accountants may choose to react to Solomon's criticisms by arguing, for example, that he is lamenting the absence of certainty in economic affairs, that he disregards several important accounting standards (verifiability, freedom from bias, quantifiability), and that he fails to draw a distinction between accounting and other functions; or we may assume that our critic means to be constructive and react to the stimulus in a positive fashion. While the former approach offers ample opportunities, it has been exploited so well by others[2] that I propose to agree with Solomon's general position and extend his argument a bit.

First, let us review the nature of the problem — the sources of errors in the computation of return on investment. Professor Solomon has concentrated on three: (1) The firm's accounting policy with respect to the distinction between expenditures to be charged to expense and those to be capitalized — the assumption being that whatever that policy is, it is not likely to achieve perfect results; (2) the failure to use up-to-date measures of the asset amount and depreciation when price levels change; and (3) errors in the measurement of the asset amount and the depreciation expense due to poor estimates of asset lives and patterns of service flows (including the failure to consider the time value of money). Solomon has also pointed out that the materiality of the discrepancy between book yield and true yield due to the omission of the interest factor from the former is affected by the lives of assets and by the firm's investment growth rate. He has

---

[1] See Ezra Solomon [3, pp. 232–44] and Ezra Solomon and Jaime C. Laya [4, pp. 152-83].
[2] Notably William J. Vatter [5].

181

found that the interest errors in a portfolio of projects net out to zero when the investment growth rate is equal to the true yield. I might add that this is not an insignificant case since such an equality occurs when all income is plowed back into new projects. This zero payout policy appears to be closely approximated by many growing firms with no long-term debt or with a constant debt-equity ratio.

The above-mentioned discrepancies between book yield and "true yield" related to fixed asset accounting can be substantial, and I do not intend to de-emphasize them. However, I should point out additional problems in the measurement of financial attributes that affect the reported return on investment. One such problem involving fixed assets relates to the effects of their tax base on their service potential. One view of the "tax allocation" issue is that a major service yielded by an asset is the tax shield it provides. The tax shield service potential may be amortized over its own readily estimated life and in the appropriate pattern independently of the amortization of the other package of service potential. If this is not done, the after-tax book yield on the asset amount will vary from the after-tax true yield. That is to say, deferring the payment of taxes increases the true after-tax yield on an investment and reduces the effective tax rate. Showing a deferred tax liability can eliminate this discrepancy between book yield and true yield on the stock equity, but only adjustment of the asset amount can eliminate the discrepancy between book yield and true yield on assets.

Unlike Professor Solomon, who remarked that we cannot get the wrong answer on working capital, I feel that we should also be concerned with the effects of our measurements of working capital items on return on investment. Receivables, for example, certainly can be a problem; witness the $71 million write-off and $111 million provision for uncollectibles by Brunswick Corporation in 1965. Marketable securities are sometimes classified as current assets and carried at amounts far from their current market values (in one recent year Owens-Illinois Glass Company included listed securities in current assets at $20,789,566, when their market values amounted to $152,357,964). I consider such a presentation to be an error in asset measurement and doubt if it was even approximately offset by an error in income measurement. Inventories, too, can cause Professor Solomon plenty of trouble. Without going into the question of how to measure inventories in order to compute "true yield," it seems safe to say that last-in first-out, and base stock methods would not be acceptable. A case in point is National Lead Company, which carries its base stocks of lead at 3¢ per pound, tin at 21¢ and antimony at 5¢, a total of approximately $22 million below current market values in one recent year, according to my usually reliable source.

The measurement of debt can also result in discrepancies between book yields and "true yields." Southern California Edison's First and Refunding Series X 7 1/8's due January 15, 1994 were issued at 100 3/4 for an effective interest cost of about 7.07%; the same company's First and Refunding Series Y 8 1/8's due October 15, 1994 were sold at par. I doubt very much if any of us would be willing to argue that two debts that differ so much in future obligations should be carried at approximately the same liability amounts (discounted at original yield rates), as they are on the balance sheet of the issuer, if we want our financial statements to reflect a rate of return on stockholders' equity that is close to Professor Solomon's true yield. Debt measurement must be chalked up as another source of difference between book yield and "true yield" on equity.

Return on investment is a well known, widely used, and informative measure of the success of a capitalistic entity. General managers, financial managers, and investors have good reason to be interested in it and concerned about its measurement. Service oriented accountants are aware of the usefulness of the ROI measure and are as much concerned about its weaknesses and limitations as is Professor Solomon, for the area of his concern is the measurement of assets and liabilities at successive dates — the heart of accounting.

AN ALTERNATIVE TO EMPHASIS ON ROI?

"The fundamental proposition of capital theory is that the value of an asset is the future payments it provides discounted at the appropriate rate."[3] This proposition applies to tangible assets or to securities and hence to the set of all securities of a firm. "In neoclassical theory the objective of the firm is to maximize its value. . ."[4] It follows that managers seek projects with (net present) value and that residual equity holders seek knowledge of the firm's net present value and changes in it over time. Managers add to the value of the firm by making investments with positive net present values. Every such investment increases the per share value of the common equity whether it requires new financing or not. The net present value approach to project analysis and the evaluation of divisional performance on the basis of residual income after deducting the cost of capital are techniques that are consistent with this view. These techniques require one crucial measure that is not required when ROI is used for project and period analyses — the cost of capital.

[3]Myron J. Gordon [2, p. 3].
[4]Gordon [2, p. 1].

ROI is a contribution measure — a measure of the return after deducting all costs except one — the cost of capital. In this respect it is similar to the elementary managerial technique of deducting variable costs from sales to obtain the contribution of the activity to fixed costs and profits — except that this latter contribution encompasses more than one specific input. Another example of a contribution measure is a shadow price — the gross value of raising a specific binding input constraint by one input unit. An even more relevant example is the investment project analysis model

$$I = \sum_{t=1}^{n} R_t \ (1 + r)^{-t}$$

(where I is the original investment, R is the periodic return, n is the life of the project in periods and r is the rate of return). Depending upon the information available in a specific situation, this model can be solved for I, R, n or r and the result compared with management's estimate. For example, if the analyst does not know the cost of capital, he can solve for r and let the manager decide whether it is sufficient, i.e., whether r is greater than the cost of capital. If the analyst does not know the life of the project, he can solve for n and let the manager judge whether the project will last that long. If the periodic flow is unknown, the analyst can compute the periodic capital recovery required to pay back the investment with interest and let the manager judge whether the periodic value of the project justifies that "mortgage payment." If the initial investment is unclear, the gross present value of the project can be computed so that the manager can make the ordinal comparison with the "unknown" investment. This model shows that we need not make an absolute measure of every relevant variable. If we can measure every variable but one and can make an ordinal measure of the remaining item against the "contribution," we can make fairly good decisions.[5] ROI is such a contribution measure which can be used effectively by a manager who can "judge" the cost of capital. Unfortunately, to be able to make the comparison accurately time after time, the manager must have a very close estimate of the cost of capital. If such a close estimate is available, it might as well be utilized in the original analysis and in the accounts along with measures of all other costs, thus permitting the application of the net present value approach that is most consistent with neoclassical capital theory.

---

[5]This point is developed clearly by Lloyd Amey in [1].

I agree with Lloyd Amey [1] that managers can make good decisions with cardinal measures of all factors except one and an ordinal measure of that one. To accountants, this means that we had better measure everything we can as well as we can; we need not worry about a shortage of candidates for the unmeasurable factor. Would it be too optimistic to anticipate the day when accountants become interested in the cost of capital and when the related measurement problems are solved to the extent that cost of capital will rank alongside labor and materials costs in a cost accounting system? Regardless of how we answer this question, accountants need not fear an absence of opportunities to enhance the value of accounting data. Eliminating the measurement errors enumerated above and those so vividly illustrated by Professor Solomon should keep the accounting profession busy for decades at its present rate of progress.

BIBLIOGRAPHY

[1] Amey, Lloyd. "On Opportunity Costs and Decision Making." *Accountancy,* Vol. LXXIX (July, 1968), pp. 442–51.

[2] Gordon, Myron J. *The Investment, Financing, and Valuation of the Corporation.* Homewood, Illinois: Richard D. Irwin, Inc., 1962.

[3] Solomon, Ezra. "Return on Investment: the Relation of Book-Yield to True Yield." *Research In Accounting Measurement,* edited by Robert K. Jaedicke, Yuji Ijiri and Oswald Nielsen. Evanston, Illinois: American Accounting Association, 1966.

[4] Solomon, Ezra and Jaime C. Laya. "Measurement of Company Profitability: Some Systematic Errors in the Accounting Rate of Return." *Financial Research and Its Implications for Management Decisions,* edited by Alexander A. Robichek. New York: John Wiley & Sons, Inc., 1966.

[5] Vatter, William J. "Income Models, Book Yield, and the Rate of Return." *Accounting Review,* Vol. XLI, No. 4 (October, 1966), pp. 681–98.